He thought of all the living species that train their young in the art of survival, the cats who teach their kittens to hunt, the birds who spend such strident effort on teaching their fledglings to fly - yet man, whose tool of survival is the mind, does not merely fail to teach a child to think, but devotes the child's education to the purpose of destroying his brain, of convincing him that thought is futile and evil, before he has started to think.

From the first catch-phrases flung at a child to the last, it is like a series of shocks to freeze his motor, to undercut the power of his consciousness. "Don't ask so many questions, children should be seen and not heard!" - "Who are you to think? It's so, because I say so!" - "Don't argue, obey!" - "Don't try to understand, believe!" - "Don't rebel, adjust!" - "Don't stand out, belong!" - "Don't struggle, compromise!" - "Who are you to know? Society knows best!" - "Who are you to know? The bureaucrats know best!" - "Who are you to object? All values are relative!" "Who are you to want to escape a thug's bullet? That's only a personal prejudice!"

Men would shudder, if they saw a mother bird plucking the feathers from the wings of her young, then pushing him out of the nest to struggle for survival - yet THAT was what they did to their children.

~Hank Rearden in *Atlas Shrugged* by Ayn Rand~

"Keep me away from the wisdom which does not cry, the philosophy which does not laugh and the greatness which does not bow before children."

~Kahlil Gibran~

"Keep away from people who try to belittle your ambitions. Small people always do that, but the really great make you feel that you, too, can become great."

~Mark Twain~

"When you plant lettuce, if it does not grow well, you don't blame the lettuce. You look for reasons it is not doing well. It may need fertilizer, or more water, or less sun. You never blame the lettuce. Yet if we have problems with our friends or family, we blame the other person. But if we know how to take care of them, they will grow well, like the lettuce. Blaming has no positive effect at all, nor does trying to persuade using reason and argument. That is my experience. No blame, no reasoning, no argument, just understanding. If you understand, and you show that you understand, you can love, and the situation will change."

~Thich Nhat Hanh~

Each second we live is a new and unique moment of the universe, a moment that will never be again. And what do we teach our children? We teach them that two and two make four, and that Paris is the capital of France. When will we also teach them what they are? We should say to each of them: Do you know what you are? You are a marvel. You are unique. In all the years that have passed, there has never been another child like you. Your legs, your arms, your clever fingers, the way you move. You may become a Shakespeare, a Michelangelo, a Beethoven. You have the capacity for anything. Yes, you are a marvel. And when you grow up, can you then harm another who is, like you, a marvel? You must work, we must all work, to make the world worthy of its children."

~Pablo Casals~

"Here's to the crazy ones. The misfits. The rebels. The trouble-makers. The round heads in the square holes. The ones who see things differently. They're not fond of rules, and they have no respect for the status-quo. You can quote them, disagree with them, glorify, or vilify them. But the only thing you can't do is ignore them. Because they change things. They push the human race forward. And while some may see them as the crazy ones, we see genius. Because the people who are crazy enough to think they can change the world, are the ones who do."

~"Think Different" Advertisement –
Apple Computers~

The world insists on achievement and progress and it is full of enmity and strife. Can you see all this and still help your children maintain their trust and hope and peace? Can you accept the world as it is yet live according to a different standard? Can you let your children see a way of living that transforms, heals, nurtures and loves? If you complain about politics and gripe about taxes and stew about the sorry state of things, your children will learn to whine instead of laugh. If you can see in every moment a chance to live, to accept and to appreciate, your children will transform the world.

~William Martin~

Foreword

Hi, it's me, "the unprocessed child." I invented that name. Several years ago a friend complimented me on my quirky handwriting, and I said, "Thanks, it's unprocessed. Untouched by the school system that shapes other kids' ABCs." Later, as Mom was searching for a title for her book, I thought of 'unprocessed' again and it seemed to fit.

You'll become very familiar with me in the following pages. My real name is Laurie, and I was earmarked to be an unschooler while I was a mere gestating fetus, but I didn't know that I was an unschooler until I was about seventeen.

I thought I was a homeschooler. When we were out in public and nosy people asked why I wasn't in school, I would say, "I'm homeschooled." I hated that question nearly as much as I hated the varying degrees of horror and condemnation that followed. I suppose that we never said "unschooled" in order to protect ourselves from being reported to some governmental agency.

We told lots of white lies. We faked progress reports to Louisiana's school board so they would leave us alone. When adults asked me what grade I was in, I would try to figure it out. I would think, *okay, first grade is six years old because Aunt Laura teaches first grade and her kids are six, so second grade is seven. I'm eight, so I'm in third grade.*

"I guess I'm in third grade," I'd respond.

Even though Mom told me that it didn't matter what other people thought, and that the school board was stupid, I started getting a little panicky when I was in my mid-teens. I had developed a conception of myself as a lazy homeschooler. I asked Mom, tearfully, why she hadn't made me learn math. She responded that she knew that I would learn it when I needed to and was ready.

"How do you know that?" I'd ask. She said it would be just like learning to read, but I didn't believe her. I thought of myself as untested, unproven, in limbo.

Then, when I was seventeen, I read Summerhill and I understood. It was amazing. I finally understood why Mom believed what she did about the nature of children. I apologized to her for being so doubtful about how I was being raised, and asked her why she hadn't explained it to me. She thought she had.

Mom's mistake was only telling me the conclusions she reached after reading Summerhill and various John Holt books. Of course she told me that all people learn different things in different ways at different times, but she didn't share the examples that led her to believe that. Mom didn't tell me about the happy, fulfilled man who had gone to Summerhill and was so completely dedicated to being a mechanic that he didn't really learn to read until he wanted to at the age of eighteen.

Here was a wealth of anecdotes about

kids who were allowed to be completely unique, just like me, outside of a mandatory school system. And they were *just fine*. In fact, they were generally happier and more successful than school kids.

More revelations came later, in the spring of 2001 when I edited the first draft of this book and got Mom's full story. She told accounts of my childhood that I didn't remember, and advanced theories that I hadn't heard. It made me realize just how radical my upbringing was, and how lucky I was to have experienced it.

I realize now that my teenage doubts were the same as the doubts that plague many homeschooling and unschooling parents. I hope that your fears will be quieted just as mine were as you read my mother's story.

Laurie Chancey

The Unprocessed Child:

Living Without School

For Laurie

"It's not really a decision... just a merge into another lane, ya know? I can get off at the next exit if I want to. Cruisin on the highway of life."

~Laurie Chancey~

〰〰〰〰〰〰〰〰〰〰〰〰〰〰〰〰〰〰〰〰〰

Acknowledgements

First of all I would like to thank Laurie's father, Arthur Wyatt Chancey. He worked many hours of overtime so that we could afford for me to stay home with Laurie. He gave me free reign to use a radical approach to child rearing that he didn't always agree with. Most of all, he said, "You were right," when Laurie reached adulthood. Without his support, the parenting path I chose would have been far more difficult.

Secondly, I would like to thank Lorne William Heibert for providing me with an idyllic setting in which to write. Lorne encouraged me and believed in my ability to put my thoughts onto paper. He said, "Get in there and write," until I had no choice.

Thank you to my sister-in-law Rebecca Lucille Chancey for giving me the book, *Summerhill* by A. S. Neill, when I was pregnant. That book enlightened me and assured my devotion to raising my child in freedom.

THE UNPROCESSED CHILD:

Living without School

Valerie Fitzenreiter

Unbounded Publications
Lake Charles, LA

First Edition © May 2003

Published in the United States by
Unbounded Publications
in Lake Charles, Louisiana.

The Library of Congress has cataloged this
edition as follows:
Fitzenreiter, Valerie.

The Unprocessed Child:
Living Without School

Valerie Fitzenreiter – First Edition
2003091803

Unbounded Publications ISBN:
0-9729416-0-4

w w w . u b p u b . c o m

Printed in the U.S.A.

Contents

Introduction

In 1979, when I first read about the concept of unschooling I was intrigued by the possibility of giving my child a life free of the boredom, frustration and pain that I experienced attending classes for twelve years.

The only reason I enjoyed school was also my major source of humiliation –the boys. I was teased mercilessly in elementary and junior high school because I was overweight. I dreaded going to school each day although I was an above-average student. Getting up early, fretting over what to wear, waiting for the bus by seven a.m., standing around waiting for class, then going to what I considered to be a waste of time. The subjects did not interest me and in too many instances the teachers did not seem to care.

In all fairness to teachers, their jobs are made too difficult by bureaucracy and rules that tend to halt any natural learning in the classroom. Their main job seems to be keeping the students quiet and in their seats. The truly good teachers, of whom my sister is one, must go through such an unbelievable amount of paperwork and regulations in order to be 'allowed' to make classes interesting. When parents participate in a positive way, it makes the teacher's job much easier, but this is seldom the case. The entire school system needs to be reworked if it is to become anything more than a babysitter/prison for the majority of the students. However, my main reason for writing this book is not to attack the school system; I am writing to share my experience in proving that school is not necessary for the positive growth of a child.

The majority of children in school will fail. They will fail to develop to the potential that they were born with and the desire to learn that they possessed during the first two to three years of their lives. They are born with an enormous capacity for learning, understanding, and creating, but they lose these qualities when they enter school. Why do they fail? John Holt says in his book, *How Children Fail,* that "children fail because they are afraid, bored, and confused."

Children are intrinsically motivated to please the adults in their lives. Their fear stems from the actions and words of the many expectations pushed on them by adults wanting them to succeed. Just the idea of disappointing their parents can lead to depression and mental anguish. Their boredom is caused by the meaningless busywork required of them on a day-to-day basis. The confusion sets in when they are told contradictions by authority figures and parents.

With this book I will attempt to disprove the theory that all children need to attend school or be "taught" under the guise of becoming educated and socialized contributing citizens in our society. I will also show the myriad of benefits to children when they are allowed total freedom in a world of rules and regulations.

Parents do not have to be rigidly qualified to unschool their children. Any reasonably intelligent parent can unschool a child if love and patience is present. There is also no need to have an unlimited income to purchase "school" paraphernalia. Unschooling is one of the least expensive alternatives to public school. The library is a wonderful, free source of information on every subject imaginable. There are countless activities that a family can take part in that are low-cost. Many unschooling families make thrift-shopping a part of their everyday existence. It becomes a game to see how little they can spend. Without the peer pressure of classmates, high-cost fashions are seldom an issue.

The vast majority of children start pre-school at the age of three. They are pulled away from the parent or guardian that they have spent their entire lives with and placed in a new situation. Their days are now divided into thirty-minute sessions of playtime, storytelling time, lunchtime, and naptime. They are taught at an early age that they are expected to act, think, and learn in one certain way. They not only have to learn whatever the teacher tells them to learn, but even when bored they must pretend to enjoy forced learning. The kindergarten experience supposedly stimulates the child's desire to learn and cultivates the skills he will need for learning in the rest of his school career. Instead it teaches them to automatically follow routines with unquestioning obedience even when these routines make no sense to them. The true aim of school seems to be conformity rather than learning. Schooled children have no say in what they do with their time; therefore they do not learn how to make choices for themselves.

Testing is not necessary with unschoolers. The parents are aware of what the children know because they spend so much time with them. In states where testing is mandatory, unschooled children tend to score in the average to above-average range, with no special preparation for the tests. Testing does not accurately show what a person knows; rather it shows how well he/she can take a test. In too many cases, intelligent children have done poorly on tests and their confidence in themselves has plummeted. Conversely, a poor student may do well on a test and then be expected to perform at this level later.

When children turn six years old, they generally enter elementary school. For the next five years, their days begin bright and early at six a.m. They put on the clothes that their parents pick out for them, eat the cereal put in front of them, and ride the bus to school. For the next seven hours the child will be expected to sit still in an uncomfortable chair while learning basically boring facts that too often do not seem to pertain to their lives at all.

Children begin to see books as a torture device used by uncaring teachers in the form of homework and book reports. If the parents do not enjoy books, it is unlikely that the child ever will. When children do not have the right to choose what they do with their own time, they become bored when no one is telling them what to do. If nonconformity begins to show, they are too often prescribed drugs to make them "fit in." Many children become shy and withdrawn or aggressive. Some find it easier to acquiesce to the teacher rather than face the consequences of rebellion.

Average fourteen-year-olds enter high school while learning to cope with changing bodies and personalities. Their teachers and parents are demanding more from them, while their friends are exerting peer pressure. They have four more years of 'hell' to face before they can get a job and become adults. An increasing number of teenagers succumb to the pressure from their classmates to use drugs as a means of escape. Their grades suffer and they become sexually active, which too often leads to promiscuity. A lack of control over their lives sometimes leads to violent aggression in the form of fist fighting and confrontations with knives and guns. A lack of self-respect and self-confidence sometimes causes them to drop out of school, and sometimes the inability to control their temper lands them in jail. If they make it through high school, they may settle for unsatisfying jobs or get married before they are ready. They feel confused, out of control, helpless, and without an objective. It may take years for them to recover from their childhood, if they ever do.

There have been many studies in homes, schools, and workplaces all with similar results. Mary Griffith says in *The Unschooling Handbook*, "people who are allowed to make their own decisions about how they behave, perform more competently and more effectively than those whose behavior is strictly controlled and judged by others." A child that has been unschooled does not see learning as something that one sets time aside for. They see learning as something that naturally happens, is worthwhile, and has no "set" time of day to occur. Unschoolers are generally more accepting of others, less interested in the status of a friend, and their self-confidence is not based on egocentricity. As John Holt said in his book, *How Children Learn*: "Birds fly, fish swim, man thinks and learns. Therefore, we do not need to motivate children into learning by wheedling, bribing or bullying. We do not need to keep picking away at their minds to make sure they are learning. What we need to do, and all we need to do, is bring as much of the world as we can into their lives. Give children as much help and guidance as they ask for; listen respectfully when they feel like talking; and then get out of the way. We can trust them to do the rest."

A. S. Neill was the owner and proprietor of Summerhill School in England, a private "freedom school" with a philosophy based upon his beliefs of the inherent goodness in children. He said in *Summerhill*: "I am only just realizing the absolute freedom of my scheme of education.

I see that all outside compulsion is wrong, that inner compulsion is the only value...if lazing about is the one thing necessary for their personalities at the moment...it is a recovery, and therefore it is necessary when it exists." Neill ran the school until his death, and now his daughter Zoe runs the school. His most popular quote among his advocates is: "The absence of fear is the finest thing that can happen to a child."

Any parent who has struggled five mornings a week to awaken an uncooperative child, get him dressed, fed, and out the door, will appreciate the lack of tension in an unschooled home. There is no alarm clock demanding that the day begin; no time schedule to follow; no dress code to follow. The day begins for the child when he naturally arises and leisurely makes his way through the morning. Some may think that this perpetuates laziness, but the total opposite has been proven. A self-governing person becomes more self-disciplined and more responsible. The unschooling lifestyle threatens people who are afraid of personal freedom and unstructured time. The mistaken notion that unschooling is "unparenting" is common among those that do not understand that many philosophies of parenting are involved in this form of lifestyle. The lives of most unschoolers are pretty relaxed since you are not trying to force the kids to do things all day long. Learning is not something that takes place separately from everything else in the lives of unschoolers. Their lives are a balance of all things that happen in life, whether they are positive or negative. Learning is a part of all of it, not separate from it.

Presence in a public institution does not insure that a child will learn. In many cases, it guarantees just the opposite. A classroom setting is not necessarily conducive to concentration or celebration of knowledge. Low morals and low morale are common in public schools, while the unschooled child develops confidence in dealing with his life. Unschooled children learn to think logically in a way that most schooled people will never understand. The typical unschooled child exhibits awareness in dealing with the "real world" that many children lose when they enter the institution of school.

One of the main benefits of unschooling is the extraordinary bond achieved with your child. You are with the child for twenty-four hours a day and the child learns your values, hopes, dreams and fears. You, in turn, *really* know your child. With no time schedule and no pressure to conform to the beliefs of others, unschooled children and their parents form relationships that have intimacy levels far above the average parent/child relationship. The mutual respect that is born from total trust in your child cannot be duplicated in any other way. The sincerity that you show your child is returned to you ten-fold.

John Taylor Gatto shocked the world in 1991 when he gave his acceptance speech as winner of New York State's Teacher of the Year

Award. As teacher of the year, he was expected to embrace the public school system in his speech. His statements made waves throughout the entire school system and homeschooling community as well.

Are homeschoolers and unschoolers a financial threat to our public school system? The answer is an emphatic NO. We continue to pay taxes that support this bureaucracy because we have no choice, other than incarceration. For many people the alternatives are inconceivable, unattractive, or unavailable.

Unschooling is not just a form of schooling. It gives your child the freedom and responsibility to choose what to do with his time. When a child has freedom from a restrictive routine and knows that you trust him implicitly, he generally lives up to that trust. Learning becomes something enjoyable to the child rather than something he is pressured to do. Unschooling is not a viable alternative for most people, because when the child is younger, one parent must stay home and be consistently patient, understanding, and have sincere love and respect for the child. Above all, you must enjoy spending time with him. The irony here is that a combination of school and poor parenting skills are generally the reason that children are not much fun to be with.

The school system is severely outdated and needs a complete overhaul to make it workable for the general population. To me, schools (the way they are run now) seem to be nothing more than cruel babysitters. When my unschooled daughter was younger, she had a poster on her wall that stated, "School is a wonderful institution...but who wants to be in an institution?" In my opinion, that poster said it all.

Parental Responsibility

"The disappearance of a sense of responsibility is the most far-reaching consequence of submission to authority."

~Stanley Milgram~

What are the responsibilities of parents? To see that their child is loved and nourished, educated and socialized and taught to respect themselves and others? Societal norms place these requirements on parents with no instructions on how best to accomplish them. New parents suddenly find themselves with an infant and only their past experiences to draw on. Their past experiences may only include their own parents blindly raising children according to how their parents raised them. Surely there is an evolution of sorts among parenting, but I don't believe that evolution is happening fast enough.

Our prisons are full of people who were raised without the type of guidance that gave them the confidence and strength to make wise choices. Therapists' offices are booked with appointments for people who have become so distraught with the daily pressures of life that they cannot function without the help of a professional and/or chemical substances. The main cause of the ailment leads to the repercussions caused by the demands of a society that is out of control.   Or is "control" the problem? Have we given the government officials so much control over our lives that we cannot even raise our own children in a way that will result in happy, confident adults? Have we bought into the system so thoroughly that we don't even question that the authority figures who make the rules and regulations have children whose lives are not lives we wish for our children to emulate?

I believe that it is our duty as responsible parents to teach our children to think for themselves. The best way to do that is to *let* them think for themselves. Yes, we must feed them and give them a home. Those are the basic requirements. But the emotional nourishment is just as important if we're going to produce a nation of healthy individuals. Sending a child off to school every morning to spend the day confined in a classroom with approximately twenty other children and an underpaid exhausted adult is not taking responsibility for a child. It is giving in to what society has dictated is a normal way to live. There are so many households that consist of two adults working fulltime in order to purchase a lifestyle that is detrimental to the family members and has few benefits. After a long day of rules and regulations in school, the child will often go home to more of the same from an overtired parent. Children need our time, love and respect, not expensive shoes and brand-name clothing. If you ask most children if they'd prefer a larger home or time with a non-stressed parent, I can assure you that their choice will not be the larger home if they have any experience with a non-stressed parent.

Somewhere along the way, priorities have become skewed. Adults will shrink with embarrassment if their vehicle isn't as nice as the neighbors, but they will feel no shame about putting their child on Ritalin so that he will conform to the standards of a classroom setting. A parent will brag about his obedient honor student and lower his voice when speaking of the child who is rebellious, independent and curious. This attitude is making robots out of the children who are too afraid to stand out and be different. It's also making the strong child feel that there is something wrong with him because he doesn't fit in. What you end up with is the same; children being forced into a mold of docility and discontent. Both types of children are consistently beat down through the years until many of them rebel in ways that will be harmful to them and others. Most will have children and continue the same style of parenting that oppressed them throughout their childhood. One of the saddest aspects of that, is most people aren't even aware of their own oppression.

I personally challenged the definition of what parental responsibility is when I made the decision to allow Laurie to be a natural learner. I spit in the face of tradition and did what was necessary to provide her with the safe atmosphere in which to grow at her own pace, experience self-discovery and be free of the enormous pressures that are amassed on the average child. It was not my responsibility to see that she followed a predetermined chart on what she should know at a given age. My responsibility was to see to it that she was free of that predetermination. I didn't feel obliged to give unknown people sitting in a school board office accurate data on what Laurie knew. In fact, it angered me that they had any say-so whatsoever on how my child was raised. The majority of school board members are simply robots raised in the system who never found the strength to think for themselves. They never ventured outside the box that was drawn for them. They never crossed the lines. Possibly there are some members who know the fallacies of a school education, but they haven't had the capability to remove themselves from the career that continues to support the erroneous belief that schools are necessary.

The therapists are telling us that we need time away from our children, that we need time to nurture ourselves. Why do you think we need this time? Is it because we were raised to conform to those same docile molds that our children are now expected to fit into? Do we need time away from our children because they are not much fun to be around due to the stress caused when a person is forced into situations on a daily basis? One thing that this lifestyle assures, is the need for more therapists in the future. I suppose its job security for a therapist to encourage people to follow along like good sheep. And maybe that's an unfair accusation towards therapists; after all, they are members of the herd, blindly following the crowd. Do you ever wonder who the leader is? Do you ever stop and think that you could stop following and start leading your own family?

Laurie celebrated anniversaries and birthdays with her dad and me. She was never left behind with a babysitter or made to feel that she wasn't welcome to join us. When she spent time with other family members, she knew that she could phone us to pick her up at any time. We let her know that we wanted her with us, that we enjoyed her company. Her presence with us was not based on convenience or our need for privacy. She was the child and her needs were our priority. We sincerely wanted her with us.

When Laurie was twelve years old, we dropped her off at her cousin's slumber party. She knew no one there except her cousin but decided to go anyway. Her father and I went to visit friends in a nearby town. Laurie phoned us after an hour and asked us if we would come get her. We didn't ask her why. We trusted that if she wanted to leave, there was a good reason. We broke our visit short with our friends and went to her "rescue." Her reasons for wanting to leave the party are unimportant. She was uncomfortable there for several reasons, none of which put her in danger. It was suggested to us that we should have made her "stick it out" and deal with the boredom and discomfort. We didn't feel the need to make her stay nor did we chide her for not being able to get along with the other girls. Laurie was not enjoying herself and forcing her to stay would not have changed that situation. I've stayed in uncomfortable situations and only become more miserable as the hours went by. Leaving the situation brought immediate relief. Why shouldn't she have the right to leave when she doesn't want to stay? She couldn't leave without our help. It was our responsibility to see to it that she had the ability to leave an uncomfortable situation.

My feelings of responsibility for Laurie were different from that of other parents I knew. They saw their role as being there to "teach their kid a lesson." I felt that she needed to know beyond a shadow of a doubt that I respected her opinions and needs, that I loved her unconditionally and that she could trust me to support her in all of her endeavors. That did not include dictating her every move and thought. It meant that I gave her the freedom to be responsible for her own thoughts and actions. I utilized no control over things that did not endanger her life. She chose her own bedtimes, clothing and interests. She made her own mistakes and no one pointed them out to her "for her own good." It was not my responsibility to point her in any certain direction. I knew that she would find her own direction and become a stronger adult because of that choice.

Becoming a parent is the largest responsibility in the world. There are many books that are devoted to the physical, nutritional, spiritual and emotional needs of a child. I must question these books though. Are the emotional needs really those of the child, or are they the needs of the parents? If they teach parents how to coerce, bend or mold a child into a responsible adult, then you can be certain the authors do not have the child's best interest at heart. The point of those books is to insure that the children fit into society's definition of normal, to make life easier on the parent. The effect is quite the opposite. It will never be easier to coerce a square peg into a round hole than it will be to just accept the fact that it's not going to fit. Accept that the square peg is beautiful just the way it is and remove the tension from your life. As responsible parents we must take a stand and discontinue the disrespectful practice of authoritative parenting. It is definitely not the best way to raise children.

Daily Life

Life is infinitely stranger than anything which the mind of man could invent. We would not dare to conceive the things which are really merely commonplaces of existence. If we could fly out of that window hand in hand, hover over this great city, gently remove the roofs and peep in at the queer things which are going on, the strange coincidences, the planning, the cross-purposes, the wonderful chain of events, working through generations and leading to the most outer results, it would make all fiction with its conventionalities and foreseen conclusions most stale and unprofitable.

~Sir Arthur Conan Doyle~

What does an unschooler do all day? There are as many answers as there are unschoolers. The one constant variable is that they are all doing what they want to do. Radical unschoolers follow their own separate paths that take them wherever they choose to go. They won't be sitting at a desk in a schoolroom doing mundane repetitive work. An adult assigned to keep them busy, quiet and alert will not guide their thoughts. A clock will not be dictating what they learn and when, when they go to the restroom, when they sleep and wake and how long they can visit with a friend. No one is telling them to sit up straight, be quiet and stay in a straight line. They are not being herded into one project after another without regard to their own personal interests.

What unschoolers are doing is living. They are deciding if they sit, stand or lay down. What they think about, what they work on and whom they talk to is at their discretion. They sleep when they are sleepy, eat when they are hungry and go to the restroom when they have the need. Most unschoolers do not worry about the time of day or night. They pursue their interests twenty-four hours a day without taking into account what others feel they should be doing. They are too busy living up to their own expectations to worry about the expectations of others. Unschoolers are forming opinions about the world and figuring out the best way to fit into that world while remaining true to their personal selves. Their belief systems are formed naturally and holistically from birth. They aren't seduced by fads, gossip or the media. They are level-headed, determined and consistent with their thoughts, words and actions.

Unschoolers see the world as a land of opportunities waiting to be discovered. They don't need to be motivated or pushed into finding their niche in life. They find it for themselves. Unschoolers have spent their entire lives doing what makes them happy so there is little chance that they will settle for anything less than their dreams. When we strive for our dreams, we push ourselves harder than what is expected. Their lives have not been restricted to what is acceptable to society. They reach far beyond the sphere of textbooks and classrooms and limits and boundaries. They know without being told that they can achieve anything they wish to achieve, go anywhere they want to go and be whoever they want to be. They are unbound by traditions and protocols. Unschoolers know who they are.

When Laurie was younger, many people asked me what a typical day was like in our home. Laurie's dad would go to work in the morning or sleep in following a night shift and I would go into the backyard to garden before the sun got too high. Laurie's bedroom window overlooked the garden so she could look outside and see me when she woke up. She would knock on the window and smile and wave at me and I would come inside to prepare bowls of oatmeal or Cream of Wheat and we would have breakfast together. After the dishes were washed we would go back outside and hang the laundry on the clothesline.

If the day was not too hot Laurie might lie on the trampoline and read a book. If the sun were too hot we would run any errands that were necessary or just stay inside the air-conditioned house. We would rent a movie, read a book (together or separately), play a game, sew, cook, paint or talk. In the warmer weather Laurie often turned on the water hose and played in the mud or we would get in the swimming pool. In the evening we would go for a walk or a bike ride.

For lunch we would prepare a pasta or green salad, usually making enough for Laurie's dad to take to work for his lunch. Our day would continue with whatever we felt like doing then we would cook supper. Since her dad worked twelve-hour shifts leftovers from supper were also packed in plastic containers. Laurie enjoyed packing her dad's work lunches and making certain that he had a piece of fruit, a bag of chips or a dessert she thought he would like.

My favorite times were when Laurie was in a talkative mood while we cooked because she would tell about some of the most interesting things she had read recently. She would imitate characters' voices and motions, remembering the script verbatim, and I would wonder if she would grow up to become an actress.

Every Wednesday we would spend the day with my grandmother. We would take Mamaw out to eat and to the park on nice days. Since Mamaw loved long car rides, several times a month we would drive the one hundred miles to my parents' home and spend the day. Laurie and Mamaw loved each other and I am so glad that we spent time with her on a regular basis. Mamaw died when Laurie was seven but she remembers her with fondness and has great memories of their times together. If Laurie had been in school she would not have been able to bond with Mamaw because she would rarely have seen her. That alone was a valid reason to keep her out of school.

Maybe the picture I just painted sounds too utopian? Too Ward & June Cleaverish? I was not wearing pearls, but I did find time to bake cookies. The stress of the average family with school-aged children was absent in our home. If Laurie wanted to do something she did it without worrying if one of her parents would degrade what she had done or complain about the messes that she made. She did not look over her shoulder wondering what would upset us or make us punish her.

I watch Laurie's calm demeanor now and wonder if it developed because of her lack of stress as a child. She was master of her own time then and she continues to be now. Her life is one of contentment because situations that cause stress for most people do not bother her.

So, what does an unschooler do all day? He lives an extraordinary life in the most logical way by keeping his feet on the ground and his creativity soaring. He encompasses thoughts and ideas with fervor and composure, reality and imagination and moderation and intensity. He becomes a part of the world while rising above it. He becomes concerned about social issues and what he can do to better the world. He empathizes with others about their plights in life. He is more well-rounded, open-minded and accepting of others than his peers. The judgments that he makes are rational and without malice. Most important of all, he faces reality with consistent optimism.

Deprogramming

"I hope you'll hear what I'm about to tell you. I hope you'll hear it all the way down to your toes. When you're waiting, you're not doing nothing. You're doing the most important something there is. You're allowing your soul to grow up. If you can't be still and wait, you can't become what God created you to be."

~ Sue Monk Kidd~

Deprogramming is a sequence of adapting phases that children go through if they have been in school and are now being unschooled. Children who have lived in a strict environment and are now living in freedom also experience the phases. Some children need considerable slack time and space to get over the period they spent in school and some will adapt readily to the emancipation and need little time to readjust. Each child is different and experiences affect him differently.

The main point is to trust that the child will do what he needs to do to readjust to the autonomy he had before attending school. This could take weeks or years depending on how deeply he was adversely affected in school and on the degree of independence he is allowed at home. If the child going through deprogramming only wants to sit around and watch television or play computer games, then that is what is necessary for him to do in order to adjust himself to a life of freedom. Sometimes a child will request a parent to schedule schoolwork because he is so accustomed to having his time controlled by someone else that he does not know what to do when suddenly faced without structure. It is important to give him the schedule if he asks for it because it is something that he wants and needs. Unschooling is all about letting the child grow naturally and if he wants the structure he should be allowed to have it. He may go through a period of unease, feeling that he should be doing something that society or the school board has labeled constructive. There are no time limits or guidelines for this adaptation because each child must go at his own pace.

In his book *Summerhill*, A. S. Neill tells of one boy among one hundred others that never attended a single class during the ten years he attended the school. At age seventeen he could barely read. When he left the school and decided on a profession he quickly taught himself how to read and perform the tasks necessary for his chosen career. He is now literate, demands a good salary and is a leader in his community. The common assumption that we must be forced to practice good habits as a child to be a responsible adult is erroneous. If a child is allowed to *be* a child, becoming a responsible adult is more likely.

The child that has been in a strictly regimented school or home will generally have a much longer recovery period before he is comfortable with himself and able to enjoy life. He has been told what to do for so long that it will take time before he can become self-motivated. He might be sullen, cranky, anxious, bored or all of these until he realizes that he truly is in control of his own time. Realizing that it is 'normal' for him to be irritable and perhaps fearful for a while and not trying to rush him through his feelings will significantly impact the depth of his recovery.

A child becomes insincere in everything he does when he is forced to keep his room tidy, be polite, and do repetitive schoolwork or other things that are not natural to him. If he is suddenly free from this coercion he at first does not believe it or know how to deal with the freedom. Expecting him to be immediately grateful and cooperative is asking for more insincerity. It is crucial in the process of deprogramming that the child is not expected to be obedient, pleasant and task-oriented because his life has just been transformed and only time and patience from his parents will prove to him that it is a genuine change.

The now-free child will gradually begin seeing life from an entirely new perspective and he will have so many choices to make every day that the experience will be overwhelming at first. He no longer has to get up early and dress for school so he can get as much sleep as he needs and wear what he chooses to wear. He doesn't have to hurriedly eat his breakfast then grab books and catch a school bus. He can do anything that he wants to do during the day without pleasing anyone but himself. While all of these things sound wonderful, it is not so easy to make the adjustment from being controlled to being free. The child has not been 'allowed' to think for himself and he will have to learn or relearn the technique before he is comfortable with it.

The Real World

"People are always saying to me, "But how will your free children ever adapt themselves to the drudgery of life?" I hope that these free children will be pioneers in abolishing the drudgery of life."

~A. S. Neill~

I heard "but that's how the real world is" so many times when Laurie was young. A vast number of people told me that I was too easy on her, too protective, and that she manipulated me. If she did not want to do something she did not do it and I did not try to push her into doing it. There were no threats, no spankings, no withholding of favors if she did not do something she had been asked to do. After all, I did not do everything that I was asked to do and as an adult I got no retribution. I felt that it was my right to say "no" if I was asked to do something I did not want to do. Children should have the same right. Why should children be expected to subjugate themselves just because they are younger? I was told that I was building a world in our home that Laurie would never be capable of leaving and she would never make it on her own in "the real world." They went on to say that her job would demand that she do something that she did not want to do, and she would push it off on someone else or get fired for not doing it herself.

When she was two years old I would pick her up and hold her if she asked me to. I was told that she was manipulating me into doing what she wanted me to do. I found that thought to be ludicrous. She was two years old and wanted her mommy to hold her and let her know that everything would be okay. If that is manipulation then we are all guilty of manipulating others to get what we want or need.

When I would mention that Laurie did not have to do schoolwork or homework of any kind, that we had no curriculum, I was told once again that she was being protected from "the real world." "She has no discipline." "She is in for a shock when she leaves home and finds out that things are not always going to be done for her." I can see where many people would feel this way but that is not how I saw it. I felt that adulthood and its liabilities would be upon her soon enough. I wanted her to have a childhood that was free of the mindless chores and responsibilities that our society has deemed necessary for us to fit into that 'normal' category. We as consumers of home decorating magazines have been convinced that our house must not look lived-in. We wear ourselves out trying to keep up this façade. There is plenty of time after your child leaves home to have your magazine-perfect interior. Enjoy your child while she is young and worry about being immaculate later. Visitors are usually more comfortable in a home that is not squeaky-clean anyway.

Laurie is self-disciplined and accountable. At different times in her early adulthood, she has taken a maximum load of classes at the university, worked full-time, overtime or part-time, and completed all assignments and bonus work for her classes. She has been in charge of running her household, which included collecting rent from a roommate, cooking, cleaning, doing laundry and paying bills. She has done all of her own shopping and maintained her vehicle. She can sew on a button or hem a garment. The best thing about her ability to handle whatever comes her way is that she enjoys it. She does not whine and complain that there is too much to do or that the work is too hard. She just does what needs doing. Laurie is not a helpless young lady with a Pollyanna attitude. She is a capable young lady with a love for life and a love for all that is included in maintaining that life. Her acceptance of the differences in the world and the people around her are one of the qualities that make her so special. She lives in the real world.

Remembering Youth

"A society in which adults are estranged from the world of children, and often from their own childhood, tends to hear children's speech only as a foreign language, or as a lie. Children have been treated as congenital fibbers, fakers and fantasizers."

~Beatrix Campbell~

Ah youth! We all remember the trials and tribulations of youth, the heartaches, the thrills, and the conquests. Or do we? Do we think of how we felt at our child's age about something he is going through now? Do we treat him like we wished someone had treated us; or do we duplicate what other adults did to us? It would be wonderful if our child did not have to go through the pain that we went through although there are some things that we cannot protect him from. However, having parents that respect him as they wish other adults had respected them can prevent much of the suffering that a child goes through.

When Laurie was a child I put things into perspective and realized that just because my parents or my friends felt that things were a certain way it did not mean that I had to agree. I found that I could make changes that were so sensible that it was glaringly obvious to me that the results would be positive. I did not have to be as uptight as most parents were. I could be understanding, not bossy, and be friends with

Laurie. She is a confident adult because she was given the respect as a child that all of us want.

We all have at least one bad memory of our childhood where an adult was cruel to us. Some of the stories I have heard from friends made tears roll down my cheeks. Teachers and coaches are notorious for saying things that wound us to our very soul. Stories about the barbaric words said by coaches, the lack of compassion shown when boys are not athletic, and the humiliation they suffered in front of their peers are common in schools. The antediluvian and cruel reasoning behind the harshness is that the treatment would 'toughen them up' and make them more able to handle strife in their world. Nothing could be further from the truth.

I still cringe when I recall the humiliation I felt from my first-grade teacher. During a test I taught the boy sitting next to me how to work a math problem. I did not know what cheating was. I just knew that I was finished with my test and he was struggling. I did what I thought was the right thing and showed him how to add. The teacher that I had adored before then, walked over with fire in her eyes, grabbed my paper and marked it with a big red "F -- For cheating on a test." I was horrified and embarrassed because I had never been chastised in front of my peers. I did not understand why she was so angry with me. If we were in school to learn, then why was it wrong of me to help my friend learn? My obedience to authority figures and my timidity anesthetized me to remain silent. This submissiveness is the antecedent to a future lived in fear and purposely introducing fear into a child's life is obscene.

I have seen adults choke up and fight back tears when they recalled incidents that happened to them in school. The atrocities committed against children by cruel coaches and teachers are deplorable. Most children are unable to overcome the helplessness that schools seem to create and encourage, but docile children are easier to control so the tradition continues. They do not grow stronger from these attacks; they harbor the hurt for the rest of their lives. Most of us manage to stuff the hurt down far enough to succeed in life, but it never goes away. One of my goals of unschooling was to insure that Laurie would never have to be treated with malice while she was a child and that she would have enough inner strength as an adult to deal with thoughtless, hate-filled people.

Empathy is a compassionate tool when dealing with others. The expression, "Put yourself in my shoes," asks that we comprehend things as the other person sees them. We cannot possibly know everything the person has been through or is feeling and we cannot know what a child is rationalizing, but we can attempt to remember how we felt as a child. Children are unable to experience empathy as well as adults. This is proven in schoolyards every day. Think of how the class bully made you feel when he picked on you. Think of how teachers embarrassed you when you did poorly on a test.

Recalling these instances may keep you from instigating the same feelings in your own children. Your child's feelings are just as real as yours were back then.

"Kids have it so easy these days." I hear this often, but nothing could be further from the truth. People who are twice your height rule your world. They look down on you and scowl if you have unwittingly done something that they disapprove of. At times those same people strike you with words, their hands, or an object that leaves red welts on your skin. When you have something important to say they will not listen and if they comment on what you have said it is generally negative or hurtful and humiliating. You are told what to do and when, what to eat and when, and laughed at if you try to do something that they do not think you can do. If you are having fun running and laughing you are told to slow down and keep quiet. You cannot go anywhere without an adult and they usually only take you places where they want to go. You have to go to bed when you are not sleepy, eat when you are not hungry, and smile when you want to cry. Being a kid is easy? I think not.

Being a child is difficult, even without parental power trips. It is not just that the world is made for larger people than you are, but that your welfare depends on those people. We all enjoy being independent and most of us are willing to fight for that freedom. Children have to fight for that independence daily with every adult in their lives. They live in a world that is dictated by adults who can overpower them physically and mentally. If they have any say in how things go it is because an adult allowed them to have it. Having a compassionate parent diminishes the amount of mental anguish a child is made to suffer.

I kept these things in mind when Laurie was irritable or pouting. I put myself in her shoes as much as possible and tried to see things from her perspective. When we were shopping and she became bored and unhappy we would go home. If there were things that I absolutely had to have I would explain that to her and then go get only those items without pausing to linger over others. I enjoyed shopping but the joy would disappear if I made her tag along when she was miserable. Future shopping trips would have been doomed from the beginning if she were made to "stick it out" on previous trips.

We found out years later that she was more than just cranky when shopping trips became too lengthy. She develops headaches and nausea when she is in a store with white floors and bright fluorescent lighting. When she was younger she just knew to complain about wanting to go home. If I had ignored her plea to leave the store I would have been forcing her to stay in places that were actually making her ill.

There are many adversities that parents cannot and should not try to remove from their child's life. Our lives are full of the need to make trivial and complex decisions on a regular basis. Children do not have to deal with the convoluted problems that many adults face, but they do have choices to make that are just as important to them. Allowing them to make these choices gives them the self-assurance and competence to make the more difficult decisions later on in life. If you listen to your child you will know which decisions he is ready to make. By age two he will most intently inform you that he wants to "do it myself." Respecting his need for independence is important.

By the same token, adding unnecessary difficulties to the life of a child causes more dissension for the child and the parent. Giving a child obstacles to overcome that are not essential is detrimental to his emotional development. Forcing him to do things that do not interest him, to perform chores that are mindless and seem to have no value to him, insisting that he hug someone that he does not want to hug, or demanding that he be well-behaved and tidy are just a few of the many painful dilemmas in many a child's life. If we allow a child to live a life free of the impediments that we have been conditioned to believe are necessary he will be free to learn the things that are truly necessary for his well being. He will learn who he is, how he feels, what he likes and dislikes, and what is really important to him.

How I wish I were as sure of myself as Laurie is. She knows without a doubt what her opinion is on a myriad of topics. I often question my decisions wondering if I made it for the right reason: is it really how I feel or is it what I know others expect of me? There is no indecisiveness in her mind because her emotional and physical growth from infancy has been directed by her, formed by her, and unbiased by the judgments of close-minded adults. She was allowed to make the inconsequential choices regarding her clothing, the condition of her bedroom, the color of her walls, and whether or not she played with the neighbor's child. All of these selections and many more led to her clarification of who she is. It may sound unbelievable that permitting her to choose her wardrobe at age two could help define who she is as an adult, but letting her make simple decisions as a child gave her the self-confidence to handle tougher problems as she matured. We can give this surety to our children and maybe they will teach us how to be clearer in our own minds.

Freedom

Without freedom other human values cannot be realized. Each human being needs freedom in order to develop his or her talents and to realize him or herself. Without freedom the human spirit languishes, culture and science decay, and the economy stagnates. The spirit needs freedom like the body needs air to breathe. Each human being is an individual with his own ideas and desires. But he is also a social being, dependent on other human beings and under an obligation to them. Freedom and responsibility are inseparable.

~Friedrich Naumann~

My personal definition of unschooling was one that appeared to be freedom without responsibility for Laurie while she was growing up. I wanted her to be free of the typical burdens of childhood, mainly the boring repetition that is so common in school. I knew that without rules regimenting every minute of her time, she would be able to pursue her own interests at the pace that was best for her. I sent a single sheet of paper to the school board once a year announcing that we were a private school, therefore they had no jurisdiction over what was taught in our home. This freed us from the worry of fulfilling schoolwork requirements for people who knew nothing about Laurie. There were no hours wasted force feeding her the information that she would learn in a matter of minutes when she decided she wanted to know it. I made myself accountable to the school board with that one sheet of paper so that Laurie could enjoy learning and educating herself.

I discovered that giving my child freedom in a home where the adults took care of the responsibilities helped her get through the struggles of adolescence with a minimum of anguish. She was absolved of the normal adversity of childhood and grew into a responsible and caring adult. I proved that individual freedom for Laurie created self-discipline, which included respecting the rights of others without repressing her.

Laurie learned of consequences to her actions naturally. No punishment was given to point out the obvious. She discovered on her own that she was unable to read a book if she tore the pages out. If she took a toy apart and didn't put it back together, she no longer had the toy to play with. If someone had said, "Well Laurie, look what you've done. You have ruined your toy and now you don't have it to play with," then her attitude would have been changed to anger at the person stating the obvious. Without the comment, she knew she was responsible for the destruction of the toy and was angry with no one. The incident stayed in its proper perspective and the broken toy was her focus, not anger at another person.

It appeared to onlookers that by giving Laurie so much control over her own direction, I was making sacrifices that went above and beyond my duties as a mother. Many of them felt the need to tell me that I needed a life outside of mothering. I never understood this pattern of thought. I made the decision to be a mother and my priority was to see to it that I did the job to the best of my ability. I never felt that I was sacrificing myself so that Laurie could be free. I embraced motherhood and felt that I was blessed with the opportunity of a lifetime. We all make choices in life and the choice I made was to be a mother. Being a mother meant freedom to me; freedom to be so in tune with a child that I knew her every want and need. Why would I give up this freedom for even an hour? I didn't need freedom from mothering; mothering was my freedom.

Give a child total freedom and he will learn total responsibility but he won't necessarily learn it the first day he has freedom. He is growing and developing into the person he will become. A child is not going to wake up one day and say, "Wow, Mom and Dad give me so much freedom; I think I'll do the dishes and the laundry today to show my appreciation." If a child has freedom all of his life he probably won't be aware of it until he's an adult. The only life he knows is one of freedom. He may compare his life with those of his friends, but the full extent of the gift he has been given will not be apparent for several years. He feels no moral obligation to appease his parents because they are good to him. He's just living and learning in the environment that has been provided for him. One day he will realize how special his childhood was, but don't expect accolades of his affection and gratitude while he is young.

In spite of my dedication to freedom for Laurie, I often thought of myself as an overprotective mother. I watched Laurie twenty-four hours a day. Keeping her safe was a priority. I was careful to keep the responsibility on myself rather than making it her duty to keep me in sight. I did not act frantic or aggravated at her for "losing" me. I never noticed any frustration on her part that I might be hovering over her and making her feel watched. When she was a teenager we talked about my over-protectiveness. She told me that it never bothered her, that in fact she liked the secure feeling of knowing that I was always there.

The point I am trying to make is that although I was protective, I did it in a way that did not make Laurie uncomfortable. I did not let her know my fears; I simply was always with her. Since there was no nagging or fear-inducing tactics on my part, she just enjoyed my company. Laurie's spirit remained intact.

Independence

"Nature never said to me: Do not be poor; still less did she say: Be rich; her cry to me was always: Be independent."

~Sebastien-Roch Nicolas De Chamfort~

The acceptance of the independence of our children is a strange phenomenon. We give our children so many mixed messages that they are not sure if we want them to be independent or not. We applaud them when they start crawling or walking, seeing their progress as another step in the maturing process. When they start climbing and reaching for "pretty" but breakable objects, we chastise them. We tell them to learn to dress themselves and then we complain about their choice of clothing. We order them to make their beds then laugh cruelly at their lack of skill. If they are always on the go as teens we gripe that they are never home, never stopping to think that home has become an unpleasant place to be. We push them to get a job or go to college, then cry when they leave home. It's truly a miracle when young adults newly on their own want anything to do with parents at all.

We all know that a newborn baby depends on an adult for all of his basic needs. He is incapable of survival without someone there to feed him. He can cry out to let us know that he is in need of attention, but he cannot verbalize exactly what it is that he needs. It is up to us to polish our intuitive abilities to provide what is necessary to keep him comfortable. Feeding, bathing, diapering and clothing are not enough though. He needs the consistency of gentle hands and soothing voices and to know that he is safe at all times. None of this information is new and for many parents the principles are learned from their parents. These needs are taken care of out of a sense of respect for the helplessness of the child. But for some reason, as soon as the infant begins showing signs of independence, the respect disappears and a distorted sense of values takes its place. The parents needs begin taking priority over the baby's.

The small child has been crying all of his life to let an adult know that he needs something, but suddenly those cries are construed as being the cries of a child who is trying to manipulate the adults in his life. He has always been curious about his surroundings, reaching for interesting objects within his grasp. The same adult that hung a mobile above his head specifically to teach him to reach is now slapping his hand for reaching out for an interesting object on the coffee table. His small and safe world is now wrought with booby traps in every direction. He wants to learn about his world so that he can survive and grow, but his attempts are constantly thwarted. Most importantly, he is on a determined path of learning. He craves knowledge about everything in his life. If a parent is respectful of the child, this desire to learn will continue and the child will never be disillusioned.

Every fiber of his being is striving to become independent and well-informed, yet that path is blocked repeatedly with slaps, fussing and the word "no." The only acts of independence he is allowed to perform are things which an adult commands or allows him to do. That is not independence at all; it is the epitome of confusion. A child is told many contradictory things in one day. He is told to grow up, but not given the chance to make any decisions on his own. If he dresses himself, he's told that his choices are not good enough; that his shorts don't match his shirt. His food and the precise time when he can eat are not his decision. All of these are things that are inconsequential in the grand scheme of life, but if he is allowed to decide for himself, the feelings of independence he would experience would give him self-confidence and a sense of accomplishment.

By far, the most fundamental of all rights taken from a child is his ability to control his own bodily functions. Too often when a child turns two-years old, one or both parents decide it is "time to potty train." Once again, the parents' needs are put first. They are tired of changing diapers so it's time to stop inconveniencing them, the neighbor's child is already potty-trained, or a nosey relative is telling them "it's time for that kid of yours to be out of diapers." None of these reasons take into account that the rate at which control over biological bodily functions develops is not on a time schedule. Some children can control urination and defecation at fifteen months old and some are not physically able until they are four years old. To expect a child to control his bladder before he has developed sufficiently is abusive. I've seen parents demoralize and shame their child in front of others because he was unable to get to the restroom in time. I've also seen an older sister helping the younger in-training sibling hide soiled pants from a parent. The look on the faces of both children told me that they feared the outcome if a parent found out. To introduce fear to a child is deplorable, but to make him fear his parent over the inability to control his biological functions is one of the most inexcusable of them all.

The amount of independence in a child when he is allowed to master the art of self-control according to his own schedule is apparent. The potty chair is in the bathroom (if one is being used), but there are no threats and no expectations voiced to the child. He makes the decision when to start using it, and sometimes does so without a parent even being aware of the fact. Chances are that he will walk into the room one day and say, "Mom, come see what I did," and his pride will be obvious. The parents are relaxed and not telling him to go to the restroom every thirty minutes. "Accidents" are treated as such and not turned into a stressful ordeal that causes shame, guilt and embarrassment to the child. The child spends no time worrying about what will happen to him if he soils his pants, but rather on activities that will bring more independence into his life.

Laurie's personal taste in wearing distinct articles of clothing began when she was a toddler. She wore frilly dresses over faded blue jeans, a pink tutu and cowboy boots and pounds of makeup or a worn-out pink skirt with gum stuck on the front for a professional portrait. I remember when we walked into the portrait studio for our appointment and saw the other children in dressy clothing, sitting on the chairs fidgeting; their mothers chiding them about getting their clothing dirty. Laurie sat down on the floor and started playing with one of the games. I watched her looking at the other children and wondered if she felt somewhat out of place in her favorite everyday skirt. The other children were watching her play and looked as if they wanted to join her on the floor, but their mothers told them to sit still. When it was Laurie's turn to have her picture taken, she jumped up onto the table and posed and smiled without being prompted. That picture is one of my favorite pictures of her. On the way home, she told me that she felt sorry for the other kids who had to wear scratchy clothes. She said, "Their smiles would be bigger if they didn't feel itchy." And to think, I had considered asking her to wear something "nicer."

Let a child choose his own clothes, what he eats and when, and the orderliness of his own room. These choices will foster independence in the child that leads to self-discipline, self-confidence and an overall feeling of acceptance. Unschoolers are able to offer even more chances to give their child an emotionally healthy existence. Bedtimes, pastimes, interests and friendships are at the child's discretion. There are no power struggles or power trips that would most certainly bring disharmony to the household. Your child will know when he has mastered something and will naturally move forward to the next conquest, with no threats or motivational talks necessary from you. It may not seem like you are affecting the length of a child's path to maturity by not allowing him to make the minor decisions when he is small. But if he is allowed to make the minor decisions he will have the experience to draw upon later to make the major decisions in his life.

Discipline/Self-Discipline

"In a free democracy like our own, we use words as arguments, not blows...If we can't convince our children with words, we will never convince them with violence."

~Swedish Parliamentary Minister~

In a home where a child is free to grow and learn at her own pace, discipline is an unwelcome intrusion into the lives of the members of the household and totally unnecessary. I realize the impact that statement will have on the adults in most traditional homes. They visualize children running wild in a chaotic and uncontrolled environment, wreaking havoc and causing general disarray. Possibly they will envision themselves slumping on the couch in total surrender to the children with bowls of food flying across the room and toys scattered everywhere.

Actually this scenario is more likely to happen in a home where strict discipline is enforced. Children living in a disciplined home are accustomed to holding their feelings inside and there is seldom a child who will not go ballistic or completely withdraw at some point in their lives because of the repression. The rebellion against this kind of control is evident in the actions of most teenagers. The rebellion is also there in the toddler years but it's easier for the parents to have power over the smaller children simply because of their size. Once a child reaches puberty and her size is almost equal to that of the parent, she becomes an unruly teenager and physical violence is often the result. By this stage, the parents have indeed "lost control."

A lack of discipline in a home does not mean that there is no order. It means that people of all ages in the home are free to decide what is important to them and are not punished for those decisions. When a child is free to do as she chooses she usually makes wise decisions. As long as she is not endangering herself or others she should be allowed to do as she pleases. I am not saying that an adult should sit slumped on the couch while bowls of food fly overhead, but in a home where discipline is at a minimum bowls of food do not fly.

By not disciplining a child she learns to discipline herself. Self-discipline is not something that will happen overnight. It takes many years of keeping quiet and patiently waiting for her to figure something out. It's so difficult at times to remain silent when you see her doing something that she will have to redo later but if you remain steadfast and allow her to make the "mistake" she will learn from it and try something different next time. Of course I am not talking about something that could harm her or others. People learn more from failures than they do from successes and if a child is able to make her own mistakes without hearing ridiculing comments from others then she will correct her mistakes and move on.

If an adult is always looking over a child's shoulder and telling her what to do she never learns to make decisions for herself. Sometimes we don't feel like waiting around for her to decide but showing patience at these times will give her more experience with making decisions. Approving of who she is and the choices she makes will show that you genuinely love her and believe in her. There will be times when she makes a decision that is not the wisest of choices. Unless she asks for your advice it's best to keep quiet and let her learn from her mistake without derision.

What does allowing a child to make decisions have to do with discipline? Discipline is scarcely disguised control. An adult wants a child to behave in a certain manner and when she doesn't the parent disciplines or punishes her with the intention that she will not "misbehave" again. More rules are made, more rules are broken and more punishment is doled out. A vicious circle is started that gives the parent a false sense of power over the child. I say that the power is false because a child is eventually going to do what she wants to do whether or not she's punished. She will simply become more devious learning to lie and hide better. Adults can choose not to see strength and independence as misbehavior and instead they can encourage the child to think for herself. A wise adult will realize that the true power lies in giving up the power and control and welcoming natural learning into the lives of the family.

There are enough rules and regulations governing our lives without having more in our homes. Every member of the family should feel that home is a safe place away from prying, hatred, dominance and judgments. If one or both of the adult members of the family make rules for the other family members to obey there is no justice and at some point along the way there will be a mutiny of sorts. Sometimes adults refuse to see it as a mutiny; instead seeing it as "kids that won't mind," if they notice it at all. In too many homes a child's opinion is unheard and unwanted causing the child to feel unimportant which in turn causes her to rebel.

Obedience is one of the most misused words in the traditional family. Parents expect obedience from their children as if they were in the military. They become the total authority in the home and allow no input from their insubordinates, the children. It amazes me when an adult gives a child no rights and no freedom to be herself and then is shocked when that child rebels against the adult. I have heard a parent tell his child the golden rule "treat others as you wish to be treated," just before he yelled at the child to go to his room. Why doesn't common sense tell him that he has just broken the golden rule while trying to teach it? Adults seem to think that a child should behave better than adults. They expect the child to behave angelically without having any say-so in how she lives her life. The average child spends a minimum of eighteen years living according to how others dictate she should live and then often enters a relationship where her spouse continues the abuse.

I am not suggesting that a child should control her parents with the sort of tyranny that most parents control their children. I am stating that in order for a home to be as tranquil as possible children should have the same privileges as the parents. Children are not innately quiet as a rule but if they are not being controlled twenty-four hours a day they are not spending most of their lives rebelling or thinking of ways to defy. Instead, they are busy discovering their interests and talents and working on them.

I have decided not to discuss all of the cons of spanking in this book because of all the literature that is already available on the topic. I will say briefly how I feel about hitting another person so that my opinion is clear on the topic. I see any type of hitting as being barbaric and unnecessary. Attempting to teach a child that hitting is wrong while you hit him has got to be the most warped method of training that has ever existed. Spanking is used when the adult loses his temper or cannot think of the correct words. Buy a dictionary and learn to articulate. Find a different way to communicate with your child other than with violence. I know that there are exceptions to every rule but with spanking the exceptions are very few. My friend Eileen told me that a swat on the rear of her autistic child was the only way she was able to convince him not to run out in traffic. She only had to do this twice and it was done after she tried everything else to stop him. She proved to me that there are extenuating circumstances in some cases. But to resort to spanking because your parents spanked or you see nothing wrong with it is a non-empathetic way of thinking and it's time for your child to stop paying for your inability to communicate.

There are so many benefits in an undisciplined and unschooled home. When adults aren't worrying all day about rules being broken they can relax and enjoy their family. The children are not worried about getting "caught" by their parents so they live truthful lives. They are not forced to lie to their parents to keep themselves out of trouble. No one is threatening or feeling threatened. There are no rigid schedules for bed, waking up, eating, studying (learning) or playing. Life slows down from the hectic pace that happens when an adult tries to control everything and everyone around them. Life becomes an enjoyable experience for the entire family.

Another benefit is that your child will become self-disciplined. She will have lived her life going after her interests. When something catches the attention of an adult and he decides he wants to learn it there is nothing that can stop him from the learning process. He is determined to know all that he can find out about the topic. It doesn't matter if other adults think his interest is strange or uninteresting. It doesn't matter how much work is involved in educating himself on the subject. He has figured out what he wants and is going after it. It's the same way with an unschooled and undisciplined child. She will get what she needs from life, if the parents back off and let her be.

It takes some courage and determination to stop the chaos in a household but it can be done if the adults living there choose to make it happen.

And it is a choice.

Respect

They mustn't know my despair, I can't let them see the wounds which they have caused, I couldn't bear their sympathy and their kind-hearted jokes, it would only make me want to scream all the more. If I talk, everyone thinks I'm showing off; when I'm silent they think I'm ridiculous; rude if I answer, sly if I get a good idea, lazy if I'm tired, selfish if I eat a mouthful more than I should, stupid, cowardly, crafty, etc. etc.

~Anne Frank~

I am not an advocate of the type of social respect that is forced on children from the time they learn to speak. Not only is it humiliating for the child, but it is one of the many unnecessary stresses that parents put on themselves. When the child answers a question with "yes" or "no," the parent responds in parrot-like form, "Say 'yes sir' or 'no sir.' "The child is getting the message that his replies are not acceptable without the added comment from the parent. The parent feels that they must be on guard at all times to assure their child has "manners."

It is annoying when an adult consistently corrects a child. Not only is the forced respect false, but it is embarrassing to the child to be corrected constantly, especially in front of others. You would not correct an adult if they did not "show respect" to another person so why should it be different when speaking to a child? The child does not see this as showing respect to the adult but as just one more rule to deal with when talking to adults.

A child learns by imitating his parents and other adults around him. If you say 'yes sir,' or 'no sir' he will use the term when and if he feels it is appropriate or when he sincerely feels like showing respect to an elder. He may never feel comfortable using the terms, but do not think of this as a strike against your parenting skills; think of it as giving your child one less hassle in a world full of regulations. It is also allowing him to be a sincere person.

I never told Laurie to say, "Please, thank you, yes sir, no sir, etc." I used those terms myself when I felt that they were appropriate. I assumed she would find her own comfort level at using these terms or not. She seldom used the terms 'ma'am' and 'sir' as a child and almost never uses them now. We have had discussions about it and she feels that it is an insincere and fake-sounding way to address people. It irked adults when she was smaller because she did not address them using an honorific, but I am not sure if they were more upset with me for not forcing her to be polite or if they just thought she lacked manners. The irony was that she saw adults as her equals and did not feel the need to address them with the 'sir' or 'ma'am' addition. She would say "thanks" or "please" if she felt the situation warranted it, but the other terms seemed superfluous to her.

The kind of respect that is necessary in a child's life is the true respect that he feels from you. If he feels he can voice his opinions and ideas without being ridiculed, he will share those with you with an honesty that will amaze. When a child's comments are laughed at in a condescending manner, he will learn to close up and remain silent. As adults, we do not appreciate someone scoffing at our opinions; children feel the same way.

I have seen a child run into a room, with excitement in his eyes and voice, telling of a brilliant idea he just had. The adults in the room know that the idea is silly and will not work, but instead of listening and giving encouragement to the child to 'give it a try and see what happens,' they laugh, tell the child he has a dumb idea, then go back to the adult conversation. I watch the child's face and body language as he walks away hurt and deflated. The parents never seem to notice the pain they have caused. Some might even comment to their child, "Get over it. It was a stupid idea." The callousness that adults often treat children with is revolting.

When Laurie was five years old, we were at my sister's home for a bridal shower. Laurie and the rest of the children played in the back yard while the women visited. In the midst of the gift-opening, Laurie came running into the room with enthusiasm, followed by the whole group of children all saying, "You're gonna get in trouble." She was wearing a white cotton dress with blue flowers that I had made for her. The skirt of the dress flared out when she spun and made her feel like a ballerina. The dress was now covered with handprints in bright purple. As she ran into the room, the women gasped and said, "Oh no!" while my smile could not have been bigger. I could see by her face that she had something to share with me and was very proud. Laurie said, "I made INK, Mom! I found these purple berries and squished them together and we can paint with it!" I said, "Would you show me how to make it when we are finished in here?" She grinned big and said, "Sure Mom!" She ran back out to the yard.

The other children watched with their mouths open. They had been certain that Laurie was going to get into trouble and were surprised that she not only did not get into trouble but also was encouraged to make the 'ink.' The women were also amazed that she was not in trouble for ruining her dress. The fate of the dress never occurred to me until I saw the looks on the women's faces and was asked, "But what about her dress?" I replied, "But she made ink! The stains on the dress are a testament to her creativity. Her creativity, self-esteem, and confidence are more important than all of the dresses in the world." The other children had on clean clothes but they missed out on making ink.

One of my neighbors was an art student in college and had three children who loved playing in the mud. It troubled me that she would complain about the messy clothing and three sets of dirty hands instead of just letting them enjoy the activity. They would make dishes from the mud and line them up on a board to dry. One day I was walking through the art building at the college and saw her in the pottery room with her clothing and hands 'muddy' from the clay. I asked her if she enjoyed working with the clay and she exclaimed that she loved it. I then laughed and said, "That must be why your kids love the mud so much. They are so much like you." She got the most thoughtful look on her face and never complained to her children about getting dirty again. The irony was so blatant that she could not ignore it.

Realizing that Laurie was more important than any thing and treating her with respect gave her a trust in me that could not have happened otherwise. If a child is punished for breaking a lamp, the message to the child is that the lamp is more important than the child is. If the child has been raised in a free environment he feels badly enough about breaking the lamp without being punished. The punishment drives a wedge between the parent and child. If the child knows that he will be punished for breaking something, he will learn to hide or lie about any future mishaps. Accidents happen to us all and it is time to stop making children pay so heavily for their innocent mistakes. The fun they were having, the laughter that was filling the room, is more important than the lamp. Lamps can be replaced, while the laughter of children cannot.

Instincts

"Intuition and concepts constitute... the elements of all our knowledge, so that neither concepts without an intuition in some way corresponding to them, nor intuition without concepts, can yield knowledge."

~Immanuel Kant~

Are we born with intuitive feelings or do we learn to be instinctive? I know that in my forty-seven years I have learned that my instincts are more often correct than in error. Too often I have second-guessed myself and realized later that my first thought was correct. When I was younger I never thought of myself as an outspoken person with nerves of steel. I was rather timid and went along with what others were doing rather than follow my instinctive feelings about any given situation.

When I decided to unschool Laurie, I had only my intuitive feelings to go by, because there were no success stories telling me of children who had been raised in this enlightening way and turned into responsible adults. I only knew that the experiences of A. S. Neill and the observations of John Holt made sense to me, and that I was going to do my best to raise my child in this manner. I did not realize when I started that my instincts would be all that I had to lean on for answers.

I now look at Laurie and know that I was right, for I see her as incontrovertible proof that going along with what everyone else does is not the best way to raise a child. I shudder to think that I might have sent her to school and been a typical parent. She could have ended up like her bored college classmates instead of sitting there taking in all of the information that is taught by the professors and retaining it. Since she did not attend school as a child and learn to memorize boring facts by repetition, she learns in a totally different way than most of us. She hears the information one time and usually remembers it.

In college, Laurie and I had a number of classes together, which meant that we were taking tests at the same time. I would study for three to four hours for a test while she simply looked over her notes minutes before the test. She made As almost every time while I made As and Bs. I would go over and over the notes writing them down five or six times to ingrain the data in my head long enough to take the test. I used memorization techniques that I learned in school while Laurie actually learned the data that was being taught. I have heard Laurie recite notes from classes that she took years ago with assurance that she remembered the details correctly. Since the unschooled mind is a logical thinking mind, if she did not remember a detail she would go with her instincts and generally be correct.

One definition of instincts that I found states: the complex and normal tendency or response of a given species to act in ways essential to its existence, development, and survival. I felt that the childhood I was giving Laurie was essential to her development, but unfortunately, many parents believe that what they are doing is for the 'best interest of their child.' I would have to add my opinion to the definition; that these tendencies are best followed when mindfully living in a natural state of being, as animals in the wild do. I am not saying that we lived in the woods with a dirt floor, meagerly scraping up an existence. We lived in the suburbs like most of the population. I am referring to my intrinsic attitude towards parenting.

Humans have put themselves in a position where survival means running to the store for milk and bread, rather than toiling in the garden for sustenance. The majority of us are about as far from natural living as we can possibly get. In my experience, unschooling and freedom parenting had to come from that place inside me where sagacity took precedence over societal norms. I felt that she had to be allowed to develop naturally without the restraints and repression that have become commonplace in most of our lives, therefore I allowed myself the freedom to give her what I thought was necessary to grandly persevere in this illogical world.

Honesty and Guilt

"The more sinful and guilty a person tends to feel, the less chance there is that he will be a happy, healthy, or law-abiding citizen. He will become a compulsive wrong-doer."

~Dr. Albert Ellis~

A child is born honest but is quickly taught the fine art of fibbing by others, first of all his parents. A child is perceptive and if you lie he will be aware of it. He may overhear you tell one person something and then you will tell it a bit differently to someone else. Or maybe you tell him that his medicine tastes good and he puts it in his mouth and discovers it is bitter. Or possibly he hears you telling the gas company that you've already mailed your payment that is still sitting on the desk. White lies are a part of everyday life. We tell them to protect someone's feelings or our own. We tell falsehoods to convince a child to swallow his medicine, or to keep the gas turned on. For whatever reason we lie, the child only knows that we lie. He cannot deduce the reason for lying and deem that it is reasonable. For whatever reason the lie was told, the child only knows that the truth was forsaken to accomplish a goal or to avoid discomfort. He will learn how to lie and eventually fine tune the lying to an art. Then he will be punished for doing something he learned from you.

Adults have told me that it's just a fact of life, "that children lie," but I do not accept this as a fact. Children are taught how to lie to make life easier and they are forced to lie to keep from being yelled at or hit. Sadly, their survival depends on dishonesty and ironically, they are punished when they are caught. I have seen a four-year old so adept at telling lies that she could get her younger sister into trouble for something that she herself had done right in front of her parents. I watched in disbelief one day when that same four-year old put something into the neighbor's mailbox then ran into her house and told her father that her friend had been the one to do it. He told her that he would buy her a bicycle the next day because he was so proud that she hadn't done that bad thing. She hugged him, then ran back outside with a smirk on her face that instantly made me think of the movie, *The Bad Seed*. She was taught a lesson that day; how to profit from lying.

In a home where there are numerous rules and trying something new is discouraged, a child will have many opportunities to lie each day. If a child gets into trouble when he breaks something, gets his clothing dirty, or eats a cookie before dinner, then he'll figure out quickly that blaming someone else is less painful for him. After all, he's seen his parents telling white lies, so it must be a perfectly acceptable thing to do. Maybe he hasn't completely figured out why he gets into trouble for mimicking the behavior of his parents, but he has gotten much better at deviousness. He'll hone the lying until he figures out what is believable and what needs adjusting. He will eventually find out that excuses work well too, so he'll spend time creating new ones.

What the parent wants is to have the child behave in an angelic fashion, always telling the truth yet never doing anything "wrong", to make the parent's life simpler. The parent erroneously assumes that if he has a list of rules that must not be broken, the child will eventually follow all of the rules and life will be pleasant and carefree. That might mean years of yelling, spanking and punishment, but this is expected in homes with healthy active children. In my opinion, the fact that it is expected is one of the saddest aspects of traditional parenting. The parenting techniques have been passed down through the generations and seldom does an adult consider challenging the tactics, even though these techniques rarely if ever accomplish the desired response.

I can hear the defiant parent now, saying that his kid behaves "because he knows what will happen if he doesn't." Simply because a child subjugates himself to survive does not mean the methods work. It may temporarily appear that the adult is in charge but the child will say anything to avoid the wrath of a parent. The child fearfully makes the decision to lie, while also fearing being caught telling the lie. If he doesn't fib, then he will also get into trouble for telling the truth. He cannot win, unless he behaves like a robot and stifles all curiosity about the world around him. And that is not winning. When a child has two choices and both of those choices cause him personal pain, he will experience a plethora of feelings ranging from anger, fear, hate, confusion and guilt.

Guilt is something that the average person faces in every facet of his life. It is used as a manipulator by parents, churches, friends and schools. The guilt insures that we behave in a certain manner according to the whim of others. At no time in our lives is guilt used to control us more than when we are children. A child is told that children in China have no food so that he will eat his vegetables. He is told that Santa Claus is watching him and he won't get any toys if he is bad. The list of "bad" things is so long that there is no way he can make it through a week without committing several acts of badness. He'll suffer through weeks of guilt about something he did then find out on Christmas morning that he got toys anyway, so someone was lying to him. Teachers tell him that he should be ashamed for not doing all of his homework or doing his best on a test. His friend tells him he is sad because he doesn't have candy in his lunch, so out of guilt he gives his candy to his friend.

When we feel guilty about something it serves the purpose of others, which is to have control over us. Parents use guilt to make a child appear to be the type of child they want. A child wants to please his parents and when he sees that he has caused a parent displeasure, he feels guilt about his actions. A parent will say how hurt he will be if his child doesn't play football. The child's choice not to play football was not made intentionally to hurt the parent. Sometimes a parent will tell his son that he will no longer love him if he dates a girl that the parent doesn't approve of. The son might defiantly date the girl long after he loses interest in her just to prove that he makes his own choices. Most of us hold on to our guilt feelings into adulthood. We feel guilty if we tell someone we can't do something for him or her on our day off, even though we need our day off for personal reasons. Guilt keeps us exhausted and stressed out until we learn to say "no" and live our lives the way that we see fit. A child cannot say "no" without getting a reprimand. He is being trained to do as he's told and not to dare think for himself.

Parents make morality an issue hoping that a child will choose the "right" path when making decisions. Children do not understand moral obligations that adults try to force on them. They need to do what comes naturally to them and form their own opinions about what they have done. Just as they will read or learn math when the time is right for them, they will adopt their own moral path to follow when they are ready. If they are not coerced, it will happen naturally; with coercion, they may live immoral lives and never understand why they are fighting a guilty conscience.

An adult sees rules as a method of teaching a child how to deal with the real world, but my wish was to have Laurie rise above how most of the world thinks and acts. I wanted her to use her time enjoying her childhood and learning what life has to offer. My desire was to remove the everyday worries from her existence so that she could use her energy to create a world for herself that was interesting and free of threats and fear. I wanted her to know how to survive in the world without resorting to dishonest methods and devious behavior.

I also wanted to be her friend; to have an open and honest relationship with her. We cannot expect our children to come to us with frank discussions if they do not trust us. I certainly would not trust someone who treated me the way most children are treated.

To ascertain for Laurie what I think should be basic birthrights for every child, I simply let go of any need for power over her. I never considered how much simpler my life would be as a mother, although parental simplicity was what I achieved. I physically and mentally created a childproof home. There were no hidden traps in the form of breakable items or asinine rules that dictated her every move. She never saw the need to lie because anything she did was accepted. I protected her from danger and let her spend her days growing up as pain-free as possible. My relationship with Laurie is based on openness and honesty. We trust each other implicitly with our most intimate thoughts and feelings.

Criticism and Sarcasm

"Criticism is an indirect form of self-boasting."

~Dr. Emmit Fox~

"Sticks and stones can break my bones, but words can never hurt me." The idiocy of this statement is appalling, because we have all been hurt by words. Some of the cruel words that were said to us as children stay with us for the remainder of our lives. I will never forget the pain of being taunted about my weight. The irony is that food was my solace so if I was teased about my weight I would eat until I hurt to help myself get past the pain. Maybe I retorted with the above statement when the cruel words were said to me, but the truth is that the words were devastating.

Criticism comes in many forms. It can be said with a smile and a hug, or with sarcasm and indifference. Constructive criticism is anything but constructive unless the berated person has asked for your comments and the comments are given with compassion. Some people are so derogatory of others that they are unaware of how often they find fault with others and how badly the words sting. Criticizing someone because you think it is for her own good is a misnomer. Admonishing under the guise of trying to help someone see the error of her ways is cruel. We all make mistakes and hopefully learn from them. If you are reprimanded because of an honest mistake, then your focus becomes the reprimand rather than the mistake and how you can correct it.

A child can be deeply hurt by criticism. She does not have the articulative abilities to defend herself. She will lash out with, "I hate you!" or "Leave me alone!" It is unfair for an adult to demean a child, then expect her to remain silent and 'take it.' The turmoil continues in the child and becomes intolerable. The pain manifests itself in outbursts of anger, violence or disobedience that may not show the true source of provocation. It may be weeks before she visibly reacts to your negative remark and you will never know what set her off.

Sometimes parents say cruel things about a child to another adult in front of the child. These parents do not seem to be aware of the impact of what they are saying. If they say it with sarcasm they think the child will understand that it is not meant literally.

For example, one day years ago I was in the doctor's office with an acquaintance and her two-year old son who sat reading quietly on the floor with a book. In the ten minutes before I was called in to see the doctor she said "He's so bad" three times, in reference to her son. The boy was doing nothing that could possibly have warranted this commentary (not that I think there is anything a two-year old could do that would warrant it). I asked her why she kept saying that and she said, "Oh, he's behaving now, but he's usually a little devil." I can only imagine how many times her son heard these words over the course of his short lifetime.

That boy was killed at age seventeen during a drug deal that went wrong. Did her remarks cause him to 'be bad?' I would imagine that a combination of comments such as that and her negative attitude about her son had everything to do with how his life ended. Parents should realize how their words affect their children. So many parents say, "He's so bad," meaning it as a teasing comment, but children do not understand sarcasm and teasing. Too often this teasing becomes more belligerent as the child grows older and turns into fierce arguments that could be avoided. It is easier to not say derogatory things like that when they are young because it eventually becomes a habit that is difficult to break. You may become desensitized to insulting your child, but it affects him every time you do it. Sarcasm hurts every relationship, especially relationships with children too young to understand the 'humor.'

Sometimes criticism is done under the guise of playful teasing and intended as humor. I am guilty of doing this so often that I am not always aware of it. I might jokingly say to a female friend, "Look at you in that short skirt. It's a good thing that you have nice legs." What I am really thinking is, "I can't believe she is going to wear that in public. That is one hideous skirt." My tone of voice implies that I might even be a bit jealous that she can wear short skirts, my words imply that she looks good in the skirt, and my thoughts speak what I truly feel. Young children cannot possibly understand the intricacy of sarcasm, much less be expected to laugh it off as comical.

Many times we are speaking what we feel to be the truth when we use derision. We hopefully convey humor by the tone of our voice, but a perceptive person knows that we are being derogatory. To avoid confrontation, she will laugh and take the insult as teasing, but she is aware of the seriousness of your comment, and generally her pride is somewhat bruised. Imagine the pain of a child with a consistently sarcastic parent. Each day must feel like a long string of insults.

I have heard that when someone degrades someone else it is so the one who degrades will look better to himself. Children's cognitive skills have not yet been fine-tuned enough to handle sarcasm and they cannot discern that it is meant as playful. Some have been teased so much that they have learned how to react in a way that will stop the teasing, but understanding it is beyond their reasoning abilities.

A child's world seems insignificant to some adults, but the truth is that he takes his world very seriously. It is often said that the attention span of a child is very short. If you watch a child doing something that he wants to do, you will see that the opposite is true. He can work intensely on a project for hours without boredom. Teasing a child about what he is working on or ridiculing the outcome of his work is torturous to him.

Laurie's childhood was purposely made free of society's ordinary, ubiquitous hang-ups. When she was four years old we were visiting at my sister-in-law's house and Laurie and her cousins were running through the house chasing each other and laughing. Laurie's skirt flew up as she ran through the kitchen and my sister-in-law said in a sing-song voice, "Ohm Laurie, I saw your panties." Laurie stopped in her tracks, gave a perplexed look to her aunt and said, "So?"

Laurie honestly did not know why her aunt said that. Of course her panties were seen; she was running in a dress. Why was that a big deal? She was confused and wanted to know why it mattered. She was aware that females wore panties and she could not get the gist of her aunt's comment. My sister-in-law was dumbfounded, and she could not get over the fact that Laurie did not have any qualms about her panties being seen. It is ironic that Laurie's aunt thought we were immoral for not teaching Laurie that it was wrong to show her underwear, while I thought her aunt was dirty-minded for thinking that there could be something obscene about seeing a four year-old's panties. She thought she would ridicule Laurie into shame, but Laurie's innocent reaction put the shame on her aunt.

Ridiculing is not just done by adults. Children in school can be cruel with stinging words. One of my brothers verbally abused me on a daily basis. If one of his friends was present, the teasing became even more brutal. I do not know if the pressures that are put on school children cause the teasing, but I feel that they do. They are in constant competition with each other for the best grades, handwriting, class participation, behavior, being the fastest or the strongest and even for friendships. To make themselves look better they cut down the others thinking that they can salvage their dignity by making another child look worse.

Boys are teased if they show signs of intelligence, have nice handwriting, can type fast, if they are polite and if they are not athletic. As they get older, if puberty does not happen at the average time, they are ridiculed in the boys' dressing room and made to feel shame for things they have no control over. Girls are mostly teased about some aspect of appearance. It is acceptable for a girl to make good grades or not want to play sports so the teasing is usually about appearances. Regardless of what we are teased about, the results are painful and cause long-lasting harm.

Emotions

"By starving emotions we become humorless, rigid and stereotyped; by repressing them we become literal, reformatory and holier-than-thou; encouraged, they perfume life; discouraged, they poison it."

~Joseph Collins~

Everyone feels the range of emotions that is common to humans. Why then are children told to keep their emotions inside? It has been proven over and over that it is unhealthy to keep your feelings inside, yet parents persist in trying to make children control theirs. Anger is a natural emotion that children are dissuaded from showing. Too many adults are not adept at showing their emotions in an honest and advantageous way possibly because of childhood repression. They hide how they really feel thinking this will cause others to assume they have no problems. Learning how to deal with anger would be beneficial to all of us. When a child is angry, telling her to be quiet or control her temper does not help her at all. There is something that is making her angry and finding out what it is and helping her work through that anger is imperative.

Sometimes Laurie 'talked back' to me in anger. I took this as a sign that I was not listening and would make an effort to tune in to what she was saying. The majority of the time I had to admit that she had every right to be angry with me. I am not perfect and had no problem admitting that to her. We worked through the anger each time and always ended up closer. The last thing I wanted was a wall between us caused by my inability to see her point of view.

Children are very perceptive and know when they are being treated unfairly. When they are being wronged and the adults in their life do not listen and concur with them about what they feel, then they begin keeping their feelings inside where they grow into the inevitable monsters of mental anguish.

One of the most inane things that I commonly see parents do is to yell at a child, "STOP YELLING!" This would be comical if it was not so sad. The same can be said when the parent spanks or hits the child to teach them 'not to hit.' What common sense justifies these situations? How can you expect a child to learn how to handle distressing situations without violence or loud voices if that is precisely how you handle these episodes? Setting a good example when your child is seemingly 'out of control' is not easy but it is the most important time for you to stay calm.

Sadness is another emotion that adults attempt to take away from children. We all have sad times in our lives, and tears help us get those emotions to the surface and deal with them openly. Telling a young boy to "be a man and dry up those tears" is one of the most ignorant things that adults say to males. Studies on death show that one of the reasons men die younger than women is because they are taught to hold their emotions in rather than dealing with them.

Tears make many of us uncomfortable because we are not accustomed to being honest about how we feel. I avoided talking about anything emotional when I could, because of the tears that flowed, until I was in my forties. A counselor taught me that the tears showed that I was human and having strong feelings about something and that they were nothing to be ashamed of. I still have work to do on this but I am improving. Thank you, Jerry LeBlanc.

I have seen Laurie talking in a classroom about someone she loved and letting her tears flow. I have such respect for her ability to do that. In one of our Women's Studies classes, our assignment was to write a paragraph on a deceased woman in our lives that we admired. Laurie wrote about her Aunt Susie and the emotions that she felt about Susie, and how much she missed her could not be hidden. At age twenty I would not have been able to let go like Laurie did. I would have gone so far as to skip the class to avoid crying in front of the other students.

Another emotion that is too often suppressed is happiness. How often have you seen children running and laughing and they are told to be quiet? This is an appalling thing for me. Seeing happy children does not bother most people, yet the parent feels the need to shush them. I sometimes wonder if the parent is upset because they have forgotten what it is like to be happy and carefree themselves. The children are hurting no one by enjoying themselves, and I would much rather see an excited and delighted child acting 'silly' than to see a child crying and miserable. It seems to me that the parent would realize the benefits of having a happy child.

Comforting your child when she is sad, respecting her when she is angry, and allowing her to show how she is really feeling are some of the most important things you can give her. You are conveying to her that she has the right to feel the way she feels, that we all have these feelings from time to time, and learning how to deal with these feelings will help her for the rest of her life. Consider all of the counseling that people go through in order to confront the emotions their parents taught them to repress as children. Some of these same people go home and tell their children to control their temper. We need to eliminate this vicious cycle. Therapists would be less necessary if children were free to emote.

It seems that patience is rare among parents these days, because there are so many things going on in our lives that take precedence over our children. Both parents usually work so that they can afford a desired lifestyle. There are always things that have to be taken care of and all too often the child's needs are pushed aside or ignored. Parents exhaust themselves trying to keep everything going.

Unschooling your child helps you slow the pace down and make him your top priority. If you nurture your child and expend the main portion of your energy on his welfare, you will be rewarded many times over. You will have a friend for life. If you lose your patience with your child, then take the time to apologize and he will see you just as you are: an imperfect human. Apologizing to a child lets him see that it is okay to make mistakes and even better to admit them.

One of my reasons for unschooling was that I wanted to raise my daughter myself rather than leave that to random teachers with whom I may or may not agree. We visited a daycare center when Laurie was four years old to see if she would enjoy spending a day or two a week there. I knew upon entering that it was not going to happen, because upon entering we saw babies left in cribs alone and crying. Children were kept with their age group doing the activity that was chosen by an adult for thirty minutes, then switched to another activity. Could this have something to do with why adults say children have such short attention spans? The adults seemed exhausted and frantic; their patience was gone and it was only nine o'clock in the morning. The children were not happy either.

Laurie was awestruck, seeing so many kids in one room and joined in on the game they were playing. She was right in the middle of her turn when the 'adult in charge' said, "Time," and everyone stopped and put things away, grumbling the entire time that "NOW, we have to read." Laurie looked at me, confused, and I asked her if she would like to go home and read a book. She smiled back, nodding, and we told the manager that we were not interested in joining. I left that place with a fear for the future of those children. The thought that most children were being put through that routine daily was difficult to fathom. How would this affect them later in life?

I assume that the adult caregivers were on their best behavior while I was there and that bothers me even more. If their lack of patience was so obvious to me, then how bad did it get after I left? I wonder what this does to the group of children. It is difficult for an adult to stay calm in the presence of another stressed-out adult, so how hard must it be for a child? Being in a situation like that for five days a week must have a deleterious impact on their future personalities. I would imagine that their lives at home are similar in stress and structure if their parents were not aware of the tension when they joined the daycare. The noise level around us was deafening at times. Learning patience is much easier when the adults in your life are calm.

Some friends of mine were visiting with me in the living room while their children were in Laurie's room playing. I could hear an argument start between the two other children over a toy car. Laurie would interject every so often with, "There are plenty of cars here," but the voices of the other two were escalating, despite her peacekeeping efforts. I could tell by the expression on my friends' faces that they were tensing up for battle. Soon the two children came running into the room yelling at their parents about the ensuing war over the car. Their mom stood up, grabbed the car and put it in her pocket and yelled at the children, "Get in there and stop that stupid fighting. See what happened now? Neither one of you gets the car. Happy?" The kids were crying and pushing each other. Laurie had entered the room quietly behind them. She was looking at me with an imploring look that said, "Make them go home, Mom."

The father remained silent when the confrontation was happening, then he looked at me with a tired look and said, "How would you handle this?" I took a deep breath because I felt like I would be interfering with the mom and was not sure how she would take it. As I spoke, the mother pulled the car from her pocket and handed it to me, and I sat it on the table in front of us.

Me: Boy, you two really are angry.
Kids: Yeah, he/she won't share.
Me: You both want to play with the same car at the same time don't you?
Boy: Yeah and I had it first.
Me: Oh, you were playing with it first then your sister wanted it?
Boy: Yeah and I wasn't through with it.
Girl: Yes you were. You put it down.
Boy: But I was going to pick it up again.
Girl: How was I supposed to know that?
Boy: I dunno. Wanna play with it when I'm through?

Girl: Yes.

Boy: Okay, I'll tell you when I'm through.

      Laurie gave me this knowing smirk then all three of the kids ran off to her room laughing. I heard the boy give the car to the girl within a minute after they started playing again. He said, "Here sis, I'm through with it now." The parents just sat there, dumb-founded, shaking their heads slowly. They asked me how I did that and I told them about active listening. The dad assured me that he would find a book and learn how.

      Even as adults, it is sometimes so easy to get caught up in the controversy going on among our children. We want them to settle their differences without involving us so that we can have a harmonious household. We lose our patience when they come screaming to us about what the other child has done, but if we scream back at them, nothing is solved and everyone involved becomes angrier. If we stay calm and offer solutions that will make a problem seem not so formidable, then future predicaments will become easier to resolve.

Friendship

"She discovered with great delight that one does not love one's children just because they are one's children but because of the friendship formed while raising them."

~Gabriel Garcia Marquez~

I was taking a psychology class a few years ago to see what the course would teach about parenting. When the three basic types of parenting were discussed, I listened intently. Authoritarian was described as a military-type style, where the parent is in total charge and demands that the children obey a strict code of discipline. Authoritative is supposedly the best style, the parents are the bosses but they have communication with the children. The third type of parenting is permissive. This is where the children make endless demands on the parents.

After listening to the descriptions of each style, I spoke up and said that there was another style and that I had used it. The professor smirked and asked me what it was, so I told him that the way I raised my daughter was a cross between authoritative and permissive. I said that she had been unschooled and that we followed no curriculum. When I told him that she was free to do as she pleased unless it infringed on the rights of others, he replied sarcastically, "I can only imagine how well she turned out."

As coincidence would have it, we had received our college annuals earlier that day and there are two pages devoted to Laurie, discussing her unschooling and high achievements in college. There is a large picture of her sitting at her computer.

I reached into my backpack and pulled the annual out, opened it to the 'Laurie' pages and said, "That's her." Until he saw Laurie's name, he was unaware that my daughter was the same person he had heard about from his colleagues. Several psychology professors were interested in her childhood and lack of any school background. The fact that she was easily maintaining a 4.0 grade point average, sociable and participated in class made her stand out from the crowd. One of her professors labeled her "My Thinker."

The professor's mouth dropped open, and he looked searchingly into my face hoping that I was joking. He started to say something several times but no words came out of his mouth. I think I noticed a twitch. He then walked back to the front of the classroom and continued teaching. His voice seemed a little weaker but that might have been my imagination. He never commented on my parenting style, never admitted that he could be wrong.

Even people who are authorities on adolescence and parenting are highly ignorant of the benefits of unschooling. It seems that they would be curious to know all that they can since it is in their field of expertise. I have found that too many of them prefer to remain ignorant and continue teaching the outdated methods of parenting, but hopefully with the help of books on unschooling and the growing number of unschoolers, their eyes will be opened and enlightenment will follow.

Authoritative parenting has missed the proverbial boat. It has not taken a child's emotional well-being into account at all, but rather it attempts to create a child who will obey quietly with few or no complaints. The parent feels justified with using manipulation, moralizing and guilt trips even when the child becomes an adult. Authoritative parenting creates children who are often docile when young, rebellious in their teen years, and struggling with various sorts of identity crisis when they are adults. One trait that stands out as common among those who are raised by authoritative parents is low self-esteem. It generally takes years to overcome the pain from a controlled childhood and discover the true self. This insidious type of parenting is so common that all of the maladies are expected and even laughed about with friends. It is the "normal" way to raise a child.

Raising a child in a way that forms a trusting bond with him is by far a more appropriate way to parent. Being a friend to your child is the most natural relationship you can have, if you can let go of the powertrip attitude that is all too common with adults. You are a parent responsible for the shaping of an innocent child. If you do this without coercion your child will give you the respect that you have given him. The bitterness that is so common in parent/child relationships will not exist and the bond that you share will grow exponentially throughout the years.

"The child must know that you are in charge." "If you let your child get away with that now, she will turn on you when she is older." "Make the rules and stick to them." "You are not being a responsible parent if you try to befriend your child." "You will do what I said because I am the parent." All of these statements give me cold chills. This philosophy has been ingrained into our heads so deeply that parents feel inadequate if they do not follow these archaic rules. It is time that these ideas became obsolete. Being a tough, unforgiving, and untouchable parent has been proven ineffective.

Adolescent psychologists warn that being too authoritarian/militaristic in your parenting style will cause children to rebel. Alarming tendencies towards violence, thievery, sex, drugs and alcohol are common. Even if your child is passive and does not openly rebel, I assure you that the battle is going on in their heads in a more private fashion. None of the rebellion is necessary, because we can be friends with our children if we give up parental power trips. Being the boss is not conducive to close friendships unless the boss is careful not to abuse the power. The child starts working to achieve independence from infancy. Many children are headstrong and stubborn and it destroys their confidence when the parents always 'win' simply because they are the parents. When the confidence goes away, the trust goes along with it.

When Laurie was twelve years old she presented me with a button that read, "Because I'm the mommy." I laughed when I saw it and said that I did not think I could wear something like that. She said, "Mom, it's just being sarcastic. I know you would never say that." We had a good laugh and I pinned it to my shirt. For several days after that, if we disagreed on something she would say, "We will do what I say because *I'm* the daughter." Laughter ensued and the disagreement was solved quickly. There have never been power struggles between us and I doubt that there ever will be any, because we see eye-to-eye on most things and do not feel the need to 'win' when we disagree.

'Winning' an argument with a child because you are bigger or the parent is hardly a triumph. You have only proven that you are physically stronger and that you are a bully and that stance does not elevate you in the eyes of your child. Children will handle this adversity in different ways. Some will grow sullen and vow to never talk to you unless they have to, and they will become silent and mistrustful towards all adults. They have learned that they cannot win or even be treated as equals, so they keep things to themselves, and that does much harm to their personal growth and development. No one, child or adult wants a friend that bullies him.

When you consistently override a child's opinions, he becomes more determined to 'win' arguments and he will take it as a challenge and disagree at every opportunity. It will not matter what he is fighting about or even if he truly thinks he is right. Competition has become the name of the game and he will continue desperately trying to prove you wrong at least once. The stress level will be high in such a home. The child thinks the parent is never right about anything, just as the parent feels the same way about the child. Tension mounts and the family members become bitter. Even if you do not notice the tension it will be there building in the child's heart, mind and body. It may manifest itself later in the form of a temper-tantrum, sulking, and/or rebellion in the form of drugs or alcohol, and in extreme cases will result in the committing of violent crimes.

My close bond of friendship with Laurie is something that I value over everything else in my life. We know what the other is thinking, feeling, and needing most of the time. It has become so common for us to finish each others' sentences that I seldom notice when it happens. The level of respect and admiration that I feel for her goes beyond anything I have ever felt before. I value her opinions and cherish our time together. Her quick wit and sharp tongue keep me laughing and on my toes. I am honored and grateful to be Laurie's mom.

Religion and Spirituality

"I personally have nothing against the man who believes in a God – no matter what God. What I object to is the man who claims that his God is the authority for his imposing restrictions on human growth and happiness."

~A.S. Neill~

My family is Methodist and we attended Sunday school and church on most Sundays. I dreaded each and every Sunday morning looking for excuses as to why I could not go to church. Feigning illness could only be used once in a while or it would lose its credibility. Many Sundays I would hide in the balcony of the church during the Sunday school hour and at times my brother joined me there. I detested wearing an uncomfortable dress and tight, shiny shoes and being forced to sit in a boring class for an hour, then having to sit through a sermon that I repeatedly tried to understand, but never could. I always felt contempt, that my parents did not attend Sunday school and my brothers and I had to.

Many children are forced to attend the Sunday morning ritual against their will. Does that make them love God and want to abide by His wishes? In my experience, it has just the opposite affect. Being forced to worship is like being forced to say, "I love you." If you do not feel it inside it is worthless. No one truly understands all that God encompasses so how can we expect a child to grasp the concept and want to be a 'good' child to please the God that he does not come close to understanding?

The Christianity that I have witnessed is wrought with guilt-causing rules that have oppressed much of the joy of life. My god is a loving god and one that supports the human decisions and mistakes that I make, knowing that I am not acting out of malice but out of innocence and ignorance. I do not make choices in life according to God's approval or disapproval, but out of my God-given sense of what is right and wrong for me. I will not judge someone for the choices that he makes in life, but instead give him support and encouragement in whatever he chooses to do. I believe that is what God would want me to do.

Hypocrisy is my biggest problem with self-professed Christians. Growing up in the Bible Belt of the Deep South, I have known many people that profess to be Christian while verbally judging, physically abusing and morally preaching to their children and peers. If they preach that we should take the Bible literally, then why do they choose to ignore the verses that tell them not to judge, not to speak against others unless they are guilt-free themselves, and to love one another without condemnation?

I had not attended church for several years before Laurie was born because organized religion has nothing to offer me. I found my god, the one who guides and directs me, only after years of personal work away from the church. I had to unschool myself in religion, just as I had to unschool myself in education, to find the Higher Power that gets me through times of strife and is with me during the good times. Therefore, I did not force Laurie to attend church or pray to someone or something that she could not possibly comprehend. We did attend the small country Methodist church that my parents belong to when we were visiting them, because Laurie enjoyed the singing. I found myself reverting to the forced smile and repressed fidgeting while we were there, making the experience barely tolerable except for singing with Laurie.

When Laurie was thirteen, a friend convinced us to attend her full gospel church with her. Laurie was looking for something to devote herself to, feeling that she did not have a conviction or a purpose in life. I now know that she was beginning the first stages of puberty and any comprehensive activity would have helped her. We attended that church for a few months and participated in a few of the organizations related to the church. I was never comfortable there but Laurie enjoyed the singing so we stayed. The services were televised and it was impossible not to notice the flamboyant preacher directing the cameramen in the balcony above us while he was preaching. The last Sunday that we attended, the collection plate was passed three times and we decided that the overt commercialism was more than we could tolerate so we discontinued going.

Life is all about choices. There are so many spiritual options that do not involve hypocrisy, hatred, judgment, guilt, and fear. Your child will discover his own spirituality when the time is right for him or he will decide not to have any spiritual affiliation at all. That does not mean that you should not attend church if that is what you have decided is right for you, but that forcing your child to attend because of your beliefs is contrary to what is natural. If a free child decides to follow in his parents' footsteps then he will be doing so of his own volition and not out of a sense of shame, guilt or a need for his parents' approval.

Questions and Answers

"As long as men are free to ask what they must, free to say what they think, free to think what they will, freedom can never be lost and science can never regress."

~Julius Robert Oppenheimer~

Questions and answers are a natural part of all of our lives. When we want to know something we look for an answer, and there are many sources from which to find answers. When your child asks you a question and you do not know the response, there are other alternatives where the child can find out the answer. If there is a computer in the home that is connected to the Internet, there are very few questions that cannot be resolved via a search engine. The library is a valuable source of information if a computer is not accessible in the home. People in the community can offer information on specific questions according to their field of expertise. We had books on varied topics on the shelves in our home, but there were many instances where we went to the library before we got Internet access.

I found that when Laurie was trying to figure out the answer to a question but did not specifically ask me, then it was best to keep quiet. Volunteering information when you are not asked is frustrating to children and adults too. They might be aware that you know the answer to the question but they want to find out for themselves, or it could be that they even know what your response would be and they want to see if their findings agree with what you would say. When they want input from you, they will ask. They also might not care what you know, but want to discover the general consensus.

On the other hand, when Laurie would ask me a question and I knew the answer, then I would respond in kind instead of saying, "Go look it up." If an adult were to ask you the question you would most likely give them the answer. Children do not want to be dumb, they have many questions and want solutions, not ignored or told to "go look it up." If the question was a complicated one, but I knew the answer, then I would offer to show her how to arrive at the same conclusion. It would be up to her as to whether or not I did show her.

Admitting that you do not know something, is nothing to be ashamed of. No one knows all of the answers, but knowing how to find them is important. Children are usually more adept at using the computer than adults and will generally have no problems using search engines. There have been many times when I could not find something I was looking for online and asked Laurie to help me. She would have what I needed on the screen in a matter of minutes. She snickered at my fear of clicking on items or trying things I had not tried on the computer. She was fearless because she understood how a computer worked.

There were times when I would watch Laurie try to figure out how to do something. It was not always easy to keep my mouth shut but I knew she would ask if she wanted my input. When she was six years old she decided to make a pillow as a gift to me using my sewing machine. She needed to change the color of the thread, but since it was a gift for me she did not want to ask for my help. I knew that I could show her how to rethread the machine in just a few minutes, but she had not asked for help so I kept quiet. She missed a step on the first try and saw the mistake she had made and corrected it. The pillow turned out well and I use it as a backrest every time I sew.

School settings discourage questions. This is true even in the college classes. How ironic that education is supposedly the purpose of schools and yet asking a question can gain disfavor from the teacher. In some instances teachers have a rigid schedule to follow and a discussion question can "waste" valuable time. Classes where open discussions are allowed are usually favorites among the students. They enjoy the learning and therefore they learn more. These classes are rare however because most teachers cannot handle their loss of control in such a room. Quiet and order are the mainstays of most schoolrooms and with so many children crammed into one room, it's not efficient to allow too many questions. My college algebra professor would yell at a student for asking a question, saying, "If you had done your homework you'd know the answer."

Rigid teachers and strict adherence to what the school system expects a teacher to do are not the only ways in which curious students are subdued. Peer influence is also responsible. Intelligence is not cool in most middle and high schools. The label of "nerd" is hard to take when you're dealing with puberty wreaking havoc on your body. If a child is unhappy at home and wants desperately to feel a sense of camaraderie with someone, he will feign ignorance regarding school topics. I can remember hiding my A papers from friends and Laurie has done the same thing in college. She was not ashamed of her intellect, but raising the grading curve does not win friends.

Curiosity is something that a child is born with. In the beginning he wants to know everything about his immediate environment. As he gets older and sees more of the world his questions become more detailed. Around two years old most children start asking the inevitable "Why?" about all that they see. It's a nerve-wracking time for parents but answering as many of the questions as possible is important. We want our children to be curious and intelligent. Squelching curiosity because it's not convenient for us is inexcusable. Saying, "I don't know" is acceptable while saying "Would you stop asking so many questions" is equivalent to telling a child to stop learning. And unschoolers know that there is no way to stop a child from learning. He may have barriers put in front of him but he'll figure out how to get around them.

Acceptance

"Stop trying to perfect your child, but keep trying to perfect your relationship with him."

~Dr. Henker~

A child is such a blessing in our lives if we allow him to be. It is far too common to see a child with parents who dislike him and treat him with contempt on a daily basis. The irony is that the parents are responsible for causing the child to be the way that he is. When a child is shown no respect day after day, certainly he will become a child who the majority of us do not enjoy being with. Telling a child, "You are bad" is the best way to insure that the child will be malevolent, because when we hear something often enough it becomes indisputable in our minds that it must be the truth. If your parent tells you that you are bad then you must be bad. Why fight it? Just go with the opinion of authority and be what your parent says you are.

A friend of mine has two children, and it has always been clear to me that she gives her daughter preferential treatment over her son. She attempts to love her son just as much, and puts much effort into proving that he is equal in her heart. However, in times of doubt and stress, the truth becomes obvious. She is much harder on him and pushes him to be someone that he is not. When he was younger, she would tell him to stop being stupid and do his schoolwork. He was

109

interested in sports and not in the least bit interested in class work, so she would deny him the right to play sports when his grades dropped to an unacceptable level according to her. The daughter excelled in class work and therefore was allowed to participate in extracurricular activities, but the son grew more and more depressed, failing two years in school. When he turned seventeen years old he ran away from home to live with a father that never had time for him when he was younger. He has much to overcome before he can be a mature adult. If he had been allowed to expend his energy in sports like he wanted to do, he would probably have done better in class work because he would have been a happier person in general. His low grades became his self-worth.

We can do our best as parents, but if we do not listen to our child we miss out on what he needs. It is our responsibility as parents to see that our child's needs are fulfilled. If we nurture him when he is younger the rewards to us are an adult child who loves us unconditionally. He has nothing to escape from and no mental anguish to overcome, and he will thrive in this world with much fewer problems than the masses. He will be confident and self-assured and need no outside approval to reach his goals in life.

I was careful not to ever say, "I like you but I don't like what you did." This is what many of the experts believe we should say, but it sends a conflicting message. We are what we do so if something we did is not liked that is part of who

110

we are. If a child throws a temper tantrum because he is frustrated and does not understand why he cannot have something, then telling him that you do not like what he did is telling him that he had no right to be upset. This makes him feel that you do not like him or respect his feelings. You may think that you are teaching the child right from wrong, but what you are really doing is undermining the child's trust in you. Small children are too young to understand and appreciate the moral reasoning behind whether or not their actions are good or bad. Approval means love; disapproval means hate.

Bedtime

"Fear defeats more people than any other one thing in the world."

~Ralph Waldo Emerson~

I can remember the agony of bedtime as a child. I would be right in the middle of reading something, watching television, or just not sleepy and the inevitable, "It's time for bed," would be said. I was blessed with parents that did not make threats and would tell me a story as I fell asleep to help me relax. But the dreaded forced bedtime was another reminder that I was not in charge of my own life. I have been in homes where the children were threatened with punishments, spankings, and loss of allowances if they did not "go to bed this instant without complaint." Many times they were right in the middle of something they enjoyed and obviously not sleepy at all. Nine times out of ten the bedtimes were necessary so they could get enough sleep before waking up for school the next morning. Other times were so the parents could have time "without the kids interfering." Either one does not induce sleepiness in an active child.

When the home is an unschooling home fixed bedtimes are not necessary. The child can make her own bedtimes according to her degree of sleepiness like adults do. Laurie would sometimes stay up really late even when she had plans early the next morning, but if she did that she generally went to bed earlier the following night to compensate. With no one telling her when to sleep she figured out her own routine. She knew when she needed sleep and she got it. If she lost a few hours sleep and could feel it the next day she would take a nap. If taking a nap was impossible because of activities going on then she would be the one to deal with her sleepiness and she had no one to blame but herself. At times she would get cranky because of a lack of sleep and I would be aware of the reason she was cranky and be extra patient. Active listening helped at these times. She would always end up apologizing for her crankiness and admit that she had not gotten enough sleep the night before.

A few weeks before Laurie started college her dad told me that I should get her to start going to bed earlier so she would be able to handle sitting in classes. She had gotten into the habit of staying up most of the night and sleeping half of the day. I told him that she was aware of how her life was about to change and that she would have to change her own sleeping schedule. He was afraid that she would be so sleepy that she would be burned out in school and end up quitting. I felt that she would do what she needed to do but I told her about his concern and she said that she realized that changes were necessary. We did not discuss it further and she continued with her late nights. The night before classes started she went to bed earlier. The natural adrenaline kept her going on her first day at school. She went to bed a little earlier that night and her sleeping schedule got in synch with her schooling demands. There are nights when she does not get enough sleep (as is normal with most college students) but she makes up for it with naps when possible.

Not having a bedtime throughout her childhood did not cause her to be a lazy irresponsible adult. It made her realize that she was responsible for getting enough sleep and that if she did not get enough it was her fault. Some parents would say that they did not want to deal with a cranky child the next day. Is not the battle the night before worse? What about the loss of self-discipline for a child when he is not allowed to self-regulate?

Adults are frequently cranky and we deal with them. If we can adjust our attitudes for a cranky adult shouldn't we be able to adjust for a cranky child? Showing patience and tolerance to a child helps them learn to use those tools when faced with adversity. When we ourselves are crabby it does not help for someone to lose patience with us because our mood worsens and sometimes our tempers flare. When we are irritable and someone handles us with a patient attitude we generally calm down and realize how we sound to others. If you can have that patient attitude when your child is disagreeable the outcome will be more pleasant. You may even discover that what your child really wants and needs is a hug and what a wonderful benefit for you both!

Laurie's lack of a bedtime did not impose upon others. Her dad was a shift-worker and his working hours varied from week-to-week. If Laurie's nighttime routine had been noisy and disturbing I would have told her that she needed to be quiet so that he could sleep. She was also expected not to make any loud, sharp noises when he had to sleep during the day. As long as she considered his need for sleep she was free to do as she pleased.

The 'experts' admonish those of us who allow our children to sleep in our beds whenever they choose to. They say that it is a mistake to ever allow your child into your bed the first time. I say that is nonsense. Laurie slept with us anytime she wanted to and did most nights until she was around eight years old. When she was ready to sleep alone she simply got into her own bed one night and said she wanted to sleep there. There were nights when she slept with us after that but they were rare.

I enjoyed having her in our bed. We would talk quietly until one of us fell asleep. She usually woke up with a happy disposition and it was a joy to see her smiling face upon waking. We read in bed and sometimes she would read one of her books aloud and I would fall asleep hearing that sweet voice. At other times I would read aloud to her until she fell asleep. When we are together now we cherish laying in bed together talking until sleep takes over.

There are things that never get said in the course of an average day. After we are settled down for the night and darkness is all around us it seems that things come to our minds that we meant to say or do. This is the perfect time to talk quietly about the day that just passed or what we want to do on the following day. Our bodies and our minds are relaxed and there seems to be a gentleness that envelops us in our sleepy states. Bedtime was when Laurie liked to give her opinion on things that had happened that day. She would summarize experiences as if she had been thinking about them for most of the day, and she possibly had been. I would not trade these memories for all of the expert opinions in the world.

I believe that the 'never let your child in your bed' theory comes from the parents needing time to themselves. With a little bit of ingenuity you can find it by going somewhere else in the house after the child falls asleep. I feel that the security a child gets by sleeping with their parents is much more important than two adults finding time alone. The nighttime can be scary for a young child and showing empathy for this fear does not make you a weak parent; it makes you a loving one.

I find that a child in the parents' bed is one of the most talked-about issues of parenting. Parents are in a quandary about whether or not the experts are really concerned about the well being of their child or if the experts are supporting the misconception that a child should cause the parents as little inconvenience as possible. When your child tells you that he is afraid in the dark alone and wants to be with you I would hope that your love and compassion for your child takes precedence over what any authority might say is best for a child.

There is also a popular method of 'training' an infant to fall asleep alone rather than be spoiled by cuddling. With this method you place the infant in the baby bed at a reasonable hour, walk out of the room, and let him cry. Most babies will cry furiously for twenty to thirty minutes the first night then fall asleep. The second night the crying is apt to last for only ten minutes. Of course this works; the child is exhausted and has figured out that you are not going to console him. He has been deserted and he knows it.

I am sorry to say that I tried this method with Laurie when she was around a year old. Yes, it worked. I paced the floor, cried my eyes out, and watched the minutes on the clock move ever so slowly, waiting for her crying to subside. For several weeks I could put her in the bed, give her a kiss and say "night night" and she would lie there until sleep took over with no crying. I missed the cuddling and I am sure that she did too but she learned that I would not be there for her at bedtime and she accepted that. Then she caught a cold and I was almost relieved. I propped myself up in bed so that I could hold her all night with her head elevated. I never "retaught" her the bedtime desertion trick. It is a cruel and harmful act that no child or parent should have to experience. That is one of the times when the experts 'won' and Laurie and I lost. I am thankful that their win was temporary and that my better judgment ruled out my trying it again.

When I looked up the bedtime desertion trick in a recent copy of the book I am discussing I noticed that on the front cover were the words, "New and updated for today's parents." I now take this to mean that parents want to devote even less time to their children and the book gives 'helpful' suggestions on how to do this. I have since learned that the author regretted his suggestion and recanted before his death.

We have all had nightmares. Even as adults it is comforting to know we are not alone when these nightmares happen and we are relieved if there is a loved one next to us in the bed. Sometimes we can laugh at these scary dreams as soon as we awaken and stop the progress of the dream. At other times the ordeal is so vivid and terrifying that we wake up sweating and crying out. Once we are fully awake and the reality of the nightmare is gone we can usually relax and fall back asleep peacefully. This is because we know it is not real but a figment of our imagination. But it is not the same for children. The dream and the fear are real and a child needs reassurance and compassion upon awakening.

When I was a child and had a nightmare I would cry out. My dad would sit beside me on the bed, rub my back gently and quietly tell me a story. He would soon put my fears to rest by making me feel protected and safe or I would have lain there awake for hours in fear of the vision returning. I handled Laurie's bad dreams in the same manner. She had many nightmares concerning the movie Gremlins. These night terrors happen when the child gets older too. The fears are usually different but nevertheless undeniable to the child. He needs to know you are there for him and that you understand his fear as ridiculing him about his anxiety builds nothing but mistrust and pain.

Laurie loved the movie Star Wars and watched it daily for several weeks. More than a year later she dreamed that some of the characters from the movie jumped out at her from behind a bush. For some reason this nightmare terrorized her and bothered her for many months. She told the dream to me several times, her eyes getting bigger as she described the attack. I have never studied dreams and do not know the reason behind the nightmare she had but I do know that her fear was unfeigned and I joined her in walking far around bushes for quite a while. One day as we approached a bush she made no move to distance herself from it. I started moving away from the bush and she pulled my arm and said, "It's okay Mom. I'm over the bush thing but thanks."

I have heard parents tell their child that the boogey man will get her if she does not go to sleep. Have they thought for one second what that kind of talk can do to the child? It is scary enough going to sleep alone in the dark without being reminded of a possible 'boogey man.' Adding to that misery is the actuality that they told their child this in front of me and other adults assuring the child that she would be the brunt of even further ridicule if she defied her parents. I have left a living room full of adults to go sit with a child in this predicament until she fell asleep. The other adults laughed at my concern but I would rather they laughed at me than the child. Besides, I am the one the child smiled at and hugged that night.

Fears and phobias have been touted in the media as problems that need to be addressed at their first appearance. Agoraphobia has become a common affliction yet it has a simple-sounding solution. It is basically a fear of being afraid and people with agoraphobia lead lives of fear hiding in their homes. It has been shown that if they face their fears until the fear dissipates then the problem would be solved. The panic attacks that go along with agoraphobia are very real and not something that the individual uses as ploys to avoid uncomfortable situations.

My sister-in-law is agoraphobic yet until I myself had two panic attacks I did not comprehend what she was going through. There was no obvious reason for my attacks. The first one happened when I was driving home from my parents' house one night. I suddenly found it difficult to breathe and it felt like the world was closing in on me. I was afraid to continue driving and pulled over. Laurie was with me and not very experienced at driving but she offered to drive until my fear passed.

The helplessness that I felt was overwhelming. Laurie brought me back down to earth by being light-hearted and silly for the next few miles. She had me laughing and relaxing enough that I soon felt secure enough to drive again. I read about panic attacks when after I had a second one and discovered that I could talk myself out of having another one. I was to mentally convince myself that I would not allow the fear so as to avoid any future attacks. A few days later the panicky feeling returned and I dissipated it with positive thoughts. I never experienced another attack but not everyone prone to panic attacks is so lucky.

I am almost grateful for these two episodes of fear. It gave me a glimpse into what my sister-in-law and others go through on a daily basis but it also made me think about what children go through when they have fears that are unwarranted to adults. As adults we sometimes laugh off these fears and refuse to acknowledge them as real to the child. This does not help the child overcome the fear but instead makes them feel ashamed for having the fear and they tend to try to hide the fear rather than be helped through it.

My panic attacks made me realize that the fear a child feels for a monster under the bed or a boogey man must be terrifying. Laurie took my fear seriously and helped me through it the best way that a teenager could, with humor. I remember feeling shame for being afraid of nothing and I told very few people about my episodes for fear of looking foolish. Imagine how a child feels when the fears that are very real to her are handled with name calling and being ignored. Being called a "scaredy-cat" is humiliating especially when the fear consumes you habitually. We cannot let our children suffer through these fears alone. They must be taken seriously so that the fears will leave and allow them to lead a secure life.

When Laurie was five years old I took her and her cousin Asher to a movie one Saturday. This was before the MPAA had developed their G-X restrictions so I asked several people about the movie, The Gremlins. Older children and adults told me that it was comedic and not scary at all for children. Unfortunately I took them at their word and we got our popcorn and a drink and settled in for a funny movie. As the movie progressed I looked over at Laurie to see if she appeared frightened. Some of the scenes seemed fairly intimidating to me when perceiving them as a five-year old. She smiled at me each time and continued watching the movie. I should have realized that she did not want to show fear in front of Asher who was two years older than her. This movie began a nightmare for Laurie that lasted for years.

The phobia first manifested itself in the bathroom. There was a wall of cabinets facing the toilet and an opaque shower curtain across the bathtub providing many hiding places for Gremlins. I went into the bathroom after Laurie did and found every cabinet door open and the shower curtain pulled to one side. I wondered what was going on and closed everything then forgot about it. A few hours later she asked me to come to the bathroom with her. Asher had gone home and we were alone in the house.

She told me that she was afraid that Gremlins were hiding in the cabinets or in the bathtub. I opened the shower curtain and we both looked inside. I then opened all of the cabinet doors and made sure they were free of the nasty little creatures. Even though we had made sure the bathroom was Gremlin-free, she wanted me to stay in there with her. I then had to go with her into her bedroom and look in the closet, under the bed, and in each and every drawer in the dresser. She was visibly shaken by this movie.

This routine continued for years. Every time that she needed to go to the bathroom she would tell me and I would go with her and open the doors and the shower curtain and wait for her to finish. I talked about what I was cooking or something I had read to try to get her mind off of the Gremlins. She could not sleep alone either so she slept with her dad and me every night. I had to regularly check under her bed and in her closet before she would play alone in her room. The closet and bedroom doors had to be left open so that she could hear me in the house. If I went outside she wanted to be told so that she could go with me.

I knew that the Gremlins were in her imagination but they were real to her. If I had not taken her seriously or laughed at her fears there is no telling how this would have turned out. I know that her trust in me would have been shaken and she would have felt that I was unsympathetic and not on her side. If she could not depend on me when she was afraid then how could she depend on me at all? It did take a long time for the fear to be relinquished but she faced that fear every time she entered the bathroom. She thanked me years later for handling it the way that I did and giving her the dignity of being taken seriously. She said that she was aware of the Gremlins being fictional but that the knowledge did not squelch the fear.

When I was six years old my family went to visit relatives. My brothers and I climbed a tree in the front yard while my dad filmed us with his 8mm camera. I was not much of a tomboy and I had never climbed a tree. However, I wanted to be in the film so I climbed to the first limb and hung on. I was in my Sunday dress and shoes. My brothers jumped down from the tree then my dad told me to jump down. I was not even a foot from the ground but I was terrified. Those twelve inches seemed like thirty-six inches to me. I pleaded with him to help me get down but he laughed and told me to "just jump" and continued filming me. I began crying and feeling fear that I would be stuck in that tree forever. He asked me if I was going to spend the night in the tree and the fear grew. My brothers were laughing along with my dad by this time. I was afraid that if I jumped down I would twist my ankle in my flimsy patent-leather church shoes.

The fear of being stuck in the tree, the anger at my dad and brothers for laughing at me, and the torture of knowing that the whole thing was on film for everyone to see was devastating. I finally mustered up enough courage to make the leap to firm ground but this memory has been etched in my mind for the past forty years. When I am in high places or elevators my chest tightens and I feel queasy. I do not know if this is directly related to the tree incident but I suppose it could be. I do not allow my fear to stop me from doing anything but it is real nonetheless. I often wondered why my dad did not help me down from that tree. I know that he did not realize the impact of that incident and I believe that he would have helped if he had known how traumatic it was for me but it was many years before I forgave him.

Chores

"The lash may force men to physical labor, it cannot force them to spiritual creativity."

~Sholem Asch~

The majority of parents say that every child should have to do chores to learn responsibility. I disagree with this widely accepted opinion because I feel that children learn to be responsible by seeing the adults around them act responsibly. I also feel that most adults do not remember how difficult it was to be a child. What we call 'play' is work to them. The stress involved in making your child do chores that she does not want to do adds more disharmony to the family. You own or rent the home you are in, not the child. Why should the child have any of the responsibility of taking care of the mundane chores required? The child will become an adult soon enough and be taking care of her own place.

Laurie enjoyed helping me do laundry, wash dishes, cook, sweep and dust when she was younger. I never asked her to do these things; she just helped because she enjoyed it and she was imitating me. She had her own clothesline under her play deck and would wash and hang out her dolls' clothing.

As she got older and discovered other interests she was no longer interested in helping me with household chores. On occasion she would sit down and help me fold clothes but that became less common as she reached her teen years. I assigned the task of emptying the small trashcans from each room in the house one day a week. At times she would jump up and empty them when I reminded her that trash pickup was the following day; at other times she would say, "I'll get it in a minute Mom." If she was involved with something interesting she would then forget and have to be reminded again. There were a few times that I became exasperated after reminding her three or four times during the day and seeing nothing happen. The few times that I did become exasperated with her I would become aware of how I was feeling and ask myself what was really going on in the situation. Her dad told me to ask myself one important question: "Will it really matter years from now if…" and I would stop worrying about the trash because the house would not cave in if the trashcans were not emptied. Several times I asked her if she would like me to empty them for her since she was so busy with something else. I would get the most beautiful smile and warmest hug from her. "Thank you Mom. I would really appreciate that."

I know that most of you are thinking that she manipulated me into doing her work for her but I see it differently. I see it as my being respectful of her. What she was working on may not have been important to me; but it was important to her. When we are concentrating on something and it is going really well the last thing we want to do is stop and do something that is not really that important to us. If it had been another adult that was supposed to empty the trash, most of us would not hesitate to offer to do the task for them. Most people think the child should not be given the same treatment in order to teach him to be responsible. There are also times when I do not get around to all of my daily chores. Should we be more forgiving of our own neglect than that of our child's?

Laurie was also assigned the task of putting away the clean dishes. I did not like this task and she enjoyed it most of the time. As she got older and the computer and her friends were getting most of her attention she would forget to take care of the dishes much of the time. I would not appreciate someone telling me to put away the dishes if I had company so I gave her the same respect. If I saw that her evening was full and that she would not have time to get to the dishes then I would generally put them away for her.

The point I am trying to make is that putting away the clean dishes to make the kitchen look tidy was never as important to her as it was to me. Even at that there were times when I did not get to the dishes as soon as I would like to. To insist that my needs should be as important (or more so) to her than her needs would not have been fair. She now lives in her own place and washes the dishes on a semi-regular basis. There is so much going on in her life that a spotless kitchen is not of the utmost importance to her.

My housekeeping skills as a teenager lacked finesse to say the least. My mother has a picture that she took of my bedroom when I was around age fifteen showing clothes hanging out of every drawer, an unmade bed and messes everywhere. I was never given chores to do in my parents' house, but I would have complained and hated doing them if they had assigned me anything to do. As soon as I got my own place at age eighteen I became concerned about how it looked. Every home I have had since then has been orderly. When Laurie was younger I did not always take care of tasks in a timely manner but things were never out of control. Both Laurie and I are proof that not making a child do household chores does not necessarily mean they will be incompetent as an adult. I learned by experience and by watching my mother in her routine, not by teaching and repetition. The desire to have a tidy home was the only push I needed.

My best friend in middle school lived with her parents and five siblings out in the country in a large home. There was always so much work to do and the children were expected to do a large portion of that work. She had to milk the cow, feed the chickens and prepare breakfast every morning before school. On weekends she was seldom allowed to have fun because of work she had to do around the house. I remember that she had to make fairly difficult curtains for all of the windows in this enormous house. All of her responsibilities seemed so unfair to me. The parents chose that lifestyle and to have such a large family so why was it up to the children to do so much of the work? She never complained about the work to her parents but I suspected it was out of fear that she would be punished or have more work assigned to her. I feel that she lost a large part of her childhood because of that. She now has a large home of her own and four children and her children are required to do what she did as a child. Her oldest son has visited in our home and expressed his dissatisfaction with the amount of work that is expected of him at home. To me it seems that just 'being' a child should have more priority than endless chores.

The rule I was proudest of not following is the "keep your room clean" rule. If I did not want to look at the messy room I would ask Laurie if I could close the door. Her room was her space and I do not think that we as parents should dictate the organization in the rooms of our children. We all enjoy a room that we can relax in without worrying about the tidiness. A child needs his own room to be a refuge where he is the final authority on how it is kept where no adult or other sibling can walk in and demand that he clean it up. I feel that a child should have his own room and not have to share with a sibling. If that is financially impossible then finding a way to divide the room or make smaller rooms is imperative. It is important for him to have a sanctuary in which to be alone with his thoughts for that is where he gets away from the pressures of other people and learns who he really is inside.

Laurie's room went through various states of array and disarray over the years. At times she loved the freedom of walking away from a play session in her room without having to clean it up. At other times she would ask me to help her straighten out the mess that was too overwhelming for her to tackle. She told me that when she looked at the mess it was impossible for her to know where to start cleaning. She liked for me to be there helping and saying what needed to be done next. I enjoyed the times we cleaned her room together. We were able to go through all of her things and sometimes she would decide to send toys and clothing to Goodwill. We did not rush, but rather we took our time and enjoyed the process even stopping so we could play with a toy that had been buried and forgotten.

There were times when I would surprise Laurie by straightening up her room while she was away from home. She would come back to an organized room with everything put away, bed made and clothing washed and folded. She told me that it was always fine with her if I cleaned her room but if she had told me not to I would have respected her decision. Some adults might think that she owed me for what I had done but I thought she should not have to pay me for something that I wanted to do. If the room had not been cleaned she would not have complained. It is not as if she demanded that I clean her room. She knew that I liked it when her room was clean and allowed me to clean it when it was bothering me. I never felt obligated to do it; I did it because I wanted to. She also did not feel beholden to keep her room clean because I liked it that way.

We talked one time about her inability to keep her room orderly. Right after it was cleaned she would tend to put things away when she was through with them. Within a week or so things would get left out and soon the room was a mess again. She was aware that she did this and it frustrated her. She enjoyed a clutter-free room but did not have the self-discipline to put things away each time. I realized that I did the same thing. I would leave one thing out then another until I had to spend some time reorganizing. I am now much better at keeping things in their places but there are times when I set something down and forget to put it away.

Children do not have to be taught organizational skills. Forcing them to be organized before they are capable of appreciating it yet will delay their discovery of the appreciation. Free children are naturally untidy. Instead they are concerned with enjoying themselves and concentrating on their interests. They do not care if their room is tidy, their clothes are clean, or if the home they live in is orderly, because it is beyond their comprehension to place high importance on neatness. It is outrageous to expect a child to remember to wipe his shoes each time he enters the house because it simply does not matter to him if the floor is clean. You can threaten and bully him into the habit of wiping his shoes but he will be acting out of fear rather than a true concern for the cleanliness of the floor. Maturity will give him respect for your need to have a clean floor but only if he is not forced to before he is capable of that type of responsibility. Then, he will be wiping his shoes out of a genuine respect for you or because he has become appreciative of a clean floor.

Maybe having a clean floor is of the utmost importance to you? You have to ask yourself if it is more significant than the emotional well being of your children and the overall harmony of the household. Constant nagging about the floor creates tension in you and in everyone else. If you cannot let go of your aversion to a less than perfectly clean floor then it would be better for you to be ever ready with a mop as opposed to making everyone else miserable with perpetual carping. The spotless floor is your obsession, not anyone else's.

My mother kept our home tidy but with a lived-in countenance. It was comfortable and I never heard her badger anyone to help her. I never considered if my shoes were dirty or if the living room looked in disarray when I did not straighten the pillows on the couch when I stood up. I had other things on my mind and would have been annoyed at Mom for suggesting I worry about the appearance of her house.

My sister and I were visiting with our parents about five years ago. Dad was working in the garden while we sat with Mom in the living room talking. After a while Dad came walking through the back door and I noticed a smile pass between them as usual. Dad was humming as he walked through the house to retrieve something from another room. He then walked back through the house on his way to the garden, and my sister noticed that he left a trail of dirt from his shoes. She asked Mom, "How do you keep from getting upset when he doesn't wipe his feet?" As Mom got up to get the broom and dustpan, she grinned and said, "You silly thing. He comes in with that dirt." Mom is wise. She knows that the harmony between her and Dad is more important than dirt on the floor.

Adult Interaction

Laurie was never sent to her room to play when adults came over. She interacted with them as equals rather than as someone she should be intimidated by. She could carry on intelligible conversations by the age of two because we never talked 'baby talk' to her as an infant. My mother commented once, "You talk to her like she's an adult when you explain things that she asks about." She said this in a complimentary way but it made me aware of another one of the typical parenting practices that I did not employ.

I had not realized until my mother made that comment that I talked differently to Laurie than most people talked to children. I always assumed she would understand what I was saying and never felt the need to qualify my comments to her. She responded appropriately, which gave me the impetus to continue talking to her in that manner. As a result she was able to converse with adults without explanations about what they were talking about. If she did not understand something that was said she would ask about it just like an adult would.

When we were out in public and an adult would ask me a question about Laurie as if she was not there, I would look at Laurie and let her have the opportunity to give the reply. After a few years of answering why she was not in school, she looked at me and said, "Mom, you tell them. I'm tired of answering this question."

Laurie's experiences with adults were positive for the most part, but if I noticed an adult infringing on her rights I would say something in spite of the dirty looks I would receive. I find it ironic that defending children is an unexpected and often unaccepted action in today's society. The majority of adults are now aware of the need to guard children against violence, yet some of these same adults see nothing wrong with emotionally badgering children. Looking at the situation optimistically I hope that it is ignorance and not loathing that allows such conduct to take place. Children need the approval of adults because to them approval means love. I did not allow adults to show disapproval of something Laurie did or said without calling it to their attention.

When Laurie was six years old she and I went to a drive-in hamburger restaurant and placed an order for lunch. The waitress that brought our burgers to the car appeared to be in her mid-forties and was wearing very short, tight black shorts, heavy makeup, and she was chewing gum with her mouth open. As she spit her gum out on the concrete beside my car, she said, "Why ain't she in school?" I replied that we were homeschoolers and she got a revolted look on her face and said, "What a loser she'll be." What overwhelming irony that was.

I have nothing against people who work in the food industry, in fact I have worked there myself, but for that woman to say Laurie would be a loser was more than I could take seriously.

Laurie and I had been verbally attacked about her not attending school so often that we were no longer shocked by negative attitudes and tended to mainly ignore them. However, this instance was so shockingly funny that all we could do was laugh. After she walked away Laurie said, "Yeah, Mom. I want to be like her," and she pretended to spit on the floor. This of course, sent us into peals of laughter that made it difficult to eat.

If a bank president had said what she did and spit her gum on the floor I would have thought the situation to be just as comedic. It was not the woman's job that caused the 'loser' comment to be so humorous, it was her words and actions.

Humor is often my saving grace and when Laurie was young it was even more valuable. It would bother me when adults spoke down to Laurie as if she were not a viable human but I seldom got angry or allowed it to ruin my day. Laughing was my way of coping with the animosity from people ignorant about what I was doing. There were adults that would take the time to get to know Laurie and fathom that the unschooling lifestyle was creditable and they were the adults that we enjoyed spending time with.

Cooking

"Research shows that you begin learning in the womb and go right on learning until the moment you pass on. Your brain has a capacity for learning that is virtually limitless, which makes every human a potential genius."

~Michael J. Gelb~

I felt that it was important to serve healthy meals. It takes more time to cook healthily than it does to use convenience foods so much of my time was spent in the kitchen. When Laurie was an infant and I was cooking I would sometimes have her in the strap-on carrier nestled against my stomach and chest or I would hold her. When this was not feasible because of the danger of her getting burned or if something required both of my hands I would place her in the baby swing and set it up where she could see me. She would swing and watch me cook.

As she got older I would put her in the high chair in the kitchen and give her kitchen implements to play with. By the time she was two she was standing on a stepstool helping me by cutting up vegetables, stirring the food that was sautéing or adding ingredients as I measured them. Soon she was doing the measuring herself and quickly learned the different sizes of measuring cups and spoons. Her favorite meal was when we made homemade pizza because there was much chopping, sautéing and 'decorating' to be done. She took great care to put only the ingredients that each of us liked on our prospective sections of pizza.

Some people were surprised when I told them that Laurie handled a sharp knife at age two. I went with my instincts and knew that she could handle it fine. She did not use the knives when she had company and was a little excited. She used them only when we were alone in the kitchen and she never cut herself. You will know instinctively if your child has the calm temperament required to handle a knife safely. If she is prone to anger and distraction then it is best to wait until she is older.

I feel that she learned some math while cooking although this was not my intent when welcoming her help in the kitchen; I just enjoyed her company. Many things that we do on a daily basis involve math in one form or another. When we built a bookcase using six-foot boards that had to be cut down to fit a certain space she figured out how much to cut from each board. No one told her to figure that out. It was something that she saw needed doing and she did it. She learned about fractions when measuring ingredients. Division was necessary when we cut a recipe in half, multiplication when we doubled a recipe.

As she reached her teen years she lost interest in cooking and became interested in other things. She still does not love cooking but she cooks at times and seems to have a natural sense for things that go well together. I often ask her to season a dish that I have made because of her ability to get the spices 'just right.' I do best following a recipe while she tends to make up her own. I would venture to say the difference is because of the unschooling, as logic comes much easier to her than it does to me.

Most of the reading material that is available on the topics of homeschooling and unschooling attempt to convey how the school subjects can be taught or learned by doing various household tasks. A good example of that is the possibility of learning math while cooking or measuring boards. I was aware of the learning that was happening while we went about our daily lives, but I was cautious not to turn our lives into school-type projects. Nothing was done for the sole purpose of 'tricking' Laurie into learning something. She helped me in the kitchen because we enjoyed it, not because I thought it was a good way for her to learn math or anything else. I wanted the entire concept of forced education out of our lives and looking for opportunities to teach while doing daily tasks would have been against that objective. Laurie learned by having fun and living, not by being taught.

Clothing and Makeup

"Imagination is more important than knowledge."

~Albert Einstein~

Dressing up in costumes or extravagant combinations of garments is always fun for children and for many adults. If you have dressed up in stylish clothing and gone out for the evening then you know that it makes you feel festive and high-spirited. I know that I feel better when my clothes fit just right and I feel that I look good in them. Children are the same way. Letting them go out in public with the costumes of their choice is a way of giving them those same high-spirited feelings.

If you watch children wearing dress-up clothes you will see pride in their eyes and in their body language. The full skirts will swish and swirl, the scarves will be thrown over their shoulders with flair and the bracelets will be clinked together for all to hear. The child will feel beautiful, handsome, dashing and self-assured. If he is dressed in the costume of a favorite character he will feel connected to that character and most likely will take on his personality. When a child dresses in clothing made for the opposite gender he should not be discouraged. Do not make a big deal out of it and it will not become a big deal.

Laurie and her friends went with me to the grocery store in their costumes many times.

145

She loved wearing a pink leotard and tutu. Feeling graceful and pretty, she would step lightly and twirl when the mood struck her. She would put bright pink circles of blush on her cheeks, ruby red lipstick on her lips and ribbons in her hair. Many times she topped off this outfit with cowboy boots. She felt beautiful like this and it never occurred to me to tell her to change into something more 'presentable.' Sometimes she wore her flower girl dress from my sister's wedding and adopted a timid attitude. At other times she would wear gaudy clothing and lots of beads and say she was a gypsy, becoming bold and friendly toward strangers. I always wondered if she chose the costume because of how she was feeling or if she felt a certain way because of how she was dressed, but I tend to think it was the latter.

I made capes for Laurie and her friends, which had them 'flying' all over the house and yard doing good deeds. They donned handmade vests when they were a rock 'n roll band playing their tennis-racket-guitars and bucket-drums with the stereo volume turned up.

Dress-up clothing lets the child pretend that he or she is someone else for a while. He can be a fireman, father, teacher or secretary in his imagination, but when he wears the clothing suited to that occupation he becomes that person. I have tried clothing on that was not 'me,' but just trying it on made me feel different inside. These little escapes from our everyday lives are healthy and the outcomes can sometimes be rewarding. For instance, trying on the uniform of a nurse may cause us to realize that we have the capability of becoming one. We can be anything we can imagine ourselves to be. The world is a source of endless possibilities instead of a place with few choices to the child that is allowed to dress-up and pretend.

I am not sure if facial makeup is still a common problem with parents and teenage daughters, but when Laurie was twelve to fourteen years old the parents of her female friends complained to me that their daughters wanted to wear makeup and they were too young. I unwittingly solved this problem when Laurie was much younger. I wore makeup at that time and she would watch me apply it carefully to my face. Children love emulating their parents so she started putting makeup on her own face. I did not make her wash it off when we left the house to go shopping or visiting.

I bought Laurie a small makeup kit for her fourth birthday and she applied her makeup several days a week. When I told her we were going to the store she would run to put on her makeup when I did. She quickly realized what an inconvenience it was and stopped wearing makeup except when she and her friends played dress-up.

When she was a teenager she used makeup again for a short while. Once again, she found the application of makeup to be too time-consuming and unnecessary. She was learning to

147

accept herself as she was without feeling the need to improve her looks with artificial means.

I do not see the harm in letting girls wear makeup. It seems to be a rite of passage for most of us, letting us feel more mature than we really are. If a girl wants to wear makeup and is not allowed to she will most likely put the makeup on after she leaves home anyway. I remember so many girls in middle school in the bathrooms every morning applying the makeup they were not allowed to apply at home. Then in the afternoons the same girls were in the bathroom cleaning the makeup off of their faces so they could go home. Vanity is a strong obsession and cannot be controlled by parents.

The majority of girls are teased about their appearances and makeup helps them feel more accepted. Their hormones and peer pressure are making them more aware of the opposite sex and they want to look attractive. If they are determined to wear makeup, finding someone to help them apply it correctly would be a supportive move.

Sports and Exercise

"Those who are more adapted to the active life can prepare themselves for contemplation in the practice of the active life, while those who are more adapted to the contemplative life can take upon themselves the works of the active life so as to become yet more apt for contemplation."

~St. Thomas Aquinas~

Our family was not sports-oriented except for Laurie's dad watching the games on television. My only regret about Laurie's childhood is that we were not active enough in our daily lives. I gardened and went for semi-regular walks but Laurie did very little in the way of exercise preferring working at her computer or reading a book. We went swimming and played the occasional baseball game but in hindsight I should have done more with her in the way of exercise. Neither of us are sports fans but if she had had an interest in any sport we would have gotten involved. Her exposure to any sports was minimal except for a few football and basketball games where my nieces were cheerleaders and to baseball games where her cousin was on the team. When her cousin Asher visited us we threw the baseball some and occasionally even played a short game.

I feel that sports are great for children if the parents do not make it so competitive that the fun is taken out of it for everyone playing. Competition is so prevalent in a school atmosphere that they do not need more of it in the games that they play. A parent taking the sport too seriously spoils the fun for the child and turns the game into a source of stress. The town I grew up in is very centered on baseball and football. Many children are coerced to play because "your dad played and it's good for you" or just because the rest of the family enjoyed attending the sports and wanted their child involved. I may have overcompensated for this by not exposing Laurie to many sports but I wish I had found a happy medium, knowing that a sedentary lifestyle is unhealthy for the body and the mind. There are many activities that do not involve competitive sports that would have given us the exercise that we needed. If I had introduced these activities as something fun to do and not something that was "good for us" then I feel certain we would have incorporated them into our lives.

Toys

"Children's liberation is the next item on our civil rights shopping list."

~Letty Cottin Pogrebin~

There have been many articles written about the importance of not segregating boys' toys from girls' toys. If the boy wants to play with a doll this should be encouraged and the boy should not be teased about his choice. He is learning how to be a nurturing parent. If the girl wants to play with trucks and cars she should not be teased either. Living in the south where macho images are prevalent it is still common to see a boy teased if he wants to play with a doll. I have seen fathers take the doll away from his son and say, "Boys that play with dolls are sissies." That reaction perpetuates the myth that men cannot be loving parents.

We decided not to make an issue of toy choices regardless of which direction Laurie chose to go. She had dolls, blocks, cars and trucks. She had a collection of Star Wars and G. I. Joe figures that went everywhere with her, and she spent hours playing with the figures in the mud. She preferred playing with the figures with her cousin Asher, but if he was not there she played alone. Asher also played with the Barbie dolls with her. Neither one of them considered that one was more male and the other more

151

female oriented because they simply enjoyed all types of play. I remember the time I bought Asher a Barbie doll and it embarrassed him because he had gotten to the age where he realized it was 'weird' for a boy to play with them.

Laurie's dad built her a play kitchen that I thought would have been the delight of any child. It was something I would have loved when I was young but Laurie played with it for a short time then lost interest. She preferred helping me in the real kitchen. The play kitchen ended up turned on its side and made into a racetrack for the Matchbox cars. It provided a raised ramp base for the speedway made from an interior door. Laurie's room was a maze of child-created roads and detours.

At times Laurie and her friends would take string and wind it around everything in the house, making it a challenge to walk from room to room. The string would become a web, a maze to tie figures to with elaborate plans for escape or a prison that would keep them in a room – making it necessary for the warden (me) to bring them a plate of food at mealtime. Blankets and sheets draped over chairs made tents in the living room. A twin mattress on the floor under the tent provided a place to lay and watch a movie – sometimes turning into their bed for the night. I shudder to think that some children are not allowed to do this because of the mess. The mess is not forever but the memories are.

My nephews are obsessed with trucks so I have not really noticed just what else is available now. When I take them shopping we go straight to the aisle of vehicles and nothing else warrants their attention. Some children love action figures that would have given me nightmares as a child. If that is what they want to play with and they are not bothered by the gruesome appearance then what harm can be done? Laurie's love of G. I. Joe figures did not cause her to feel like shooting people.

There are very few toy purchases that I would justify now including many of the ones that Laurie was given. The toys that she enjoyed the most were the ones that required her to use her imagination. If I were to furnish a toy room for a child now the only things I would buy would be a few dolls, cars, action figures and blocks. If a child wants a tea party then real dishes can be used. Boxes, string and tape are more fun than most toys on the market and they are inexpensive items that most of us have around our homes. Large toy stores and the media have made us think our children need every new thing that becomes available. Children are happier with less.

Most toys are recommended for a certain age range and sometimes it is because there are small parts that might be dangerous to a young child. The majority of the recommendations suggest that some games and toys are too mentally advanced for him. I believe that these age restrictions should be ignored and each child's level of interest taken into account. Laurie was advanced in her puzzle-solving abilities and could work most puzzles appropriate to her age level in a few minutes. She needed the challenge of puzzles fashioned for adults to hold her interest.

Many of the toys offered are so flimsy and poorly made that playing with them at all destroys them. If a child wants to make necklaces with beads, then buying beads in a hobby store would make more sense than buying a kit from the toy department. The results will be more professional looking and the 'real' supplies are usually easier to work with and very often less expensive. So many toys seem to be made with no thought of actually being used.

Just as Laurie preferred working in the real kitchen as opposed to 'playing' at the kitchen her dad built for her, she preferred real tools to plastic ones. The little plastic tools that are sold in the toy department are useless. Children do not want something that is brightly colored and will not do the same thing that their parents' tools will do. They want to nail actual nails into real boards and create something unique or they want to use a real screwdriver and screws.

Laurie preferred helping me paint a table rather than finger painting on a sheet of paper. Finger painting seems to be a rite of passage for children but I seldom see any of them truly enjoy the process. They enjoy getting their fingers dirty but the creativity is somewhat limited. There are children that enjoy painting and they should have the proper materials to paint with. Their artwork should be taken seriously and not treated as 'play.'

I gave Laurie and Asher an old telephone and some tools one time, and while she enjoyed watching Asher take the telephone apart, she was not inclined to participate. I took that as a sign that she was not mechanically inclined and naively thought I had proven that with her lack of interest in working on the telephone. Ten years later she had assembled three computers, installed various modules and carried a small toolkit in her backpack on a daily basis, always ready when a tool was needed. The university's thermostat knobs are usually removed to only give maintenance persons control over the temperature in each room, but Laurie used a screwdriver attachment to adjust the temperature to the satisfaction of the classroom.

Laurie is also the member of the household to call on when something is wrong with any of the electronic equipment. I am intimidated by anything electrical, but she looks at the problem and usually has it working in a few minutes. I am not saying that she is an electronics genius but her sense of logic allows her to understand and fix small problems.

Vacations

It was nice to be free to travel at any time of the year without having to wait for school holidays. Laurie and I often drove the one hundred miles to my parents' house in the middle of the week. When my mother had surgery and needed my help for two weeks there was no problem because Laurie and I were able to stay there without worrying about homework or missed classes. We were not financially able to travel as much as we wanted to but the school schedule was never a factor. We could travel more than traditional families in the same income bracket because motels, amusement parks and other vacation attractions are less expensive and less crowded in the off-season. An unschooling lifestyle does not interfere with vacations.

Vacations were also a time to expand on Laurie's interests. My sister and I took Laurie on a trip to southern Missouri to visit the Laura Ingalls Wilder museum and tour the home that Laura and her husband Almanzo lived in until their death. We saw Pa's fiddle, Ma's sewing machine and many other possessions that Laurie knew about from her intense study of the Little House books. We sat in chairs with very short legs that Almanzo had built especially for Laura who was of small stature, saw the library where Laura worked and listened to an interview with her when she was in her late 80s. We visited the cemetery where Laura, Almanzo and their daughter Rose were buried. That trip made the Ingalls family even more real for us.

Two years later Laurie, her dad and I made a trip to Malone, New York and toured Almanzo's childhood home. We had a guide that took us from room-to-room and explained what everything was. Laurie corrected him on a few details and he ended up admitting that he had never read the Little House books and asked Laurie if she would consider being a guide. The request was flattering to her but we were unable to relocate to New York.

Looking back on Laurie's childhood I wish that we had traveled more but I am thankful that we were able to visit the places that we did. Seeing, touching and being in the actual places where the Wilders' lived brought the stories of their hardships to life. Laurie visited those places in her imagination first then was fortunate enough to visit them in person.

All types of vacations offer more educational opportunities than sitting in a schoolroom but the emphasis should not be on education. Not everyone can afford trips abroad to observe peoples in other countries but most can afford a trip a neighboring state. Some unschooling families take bicycle or hiking trips, keeping costs to a minimum. The restrictions for an unschooling family do not include worrying about missing school or being able to keep up with the other students.

Censorship

"Free the mind, and the intellect will follow."

~A. S. Neill~

The topic of censorship was a difficult one for me to write about. I grew up in a home where nothing 'offensive' was open for discussion, and my ignorance about so many issues caused me much embarrassment as a teenager and young adult. I was against censoring Laurie but her dad was adamant about it. I defied him about many things while Laurie was growing up but for some reason I went along with the censoring wishing later that I had not. By the time she was in her late teens his rigidity had affected me and I began feeling uncomfortable letting her see some television shows in his presence. I allowed her to watch them when he was working but this also caused me some discomfort. I did not realize until years later that his censorship in her life was affecting her and me the way my parents' censorship had; it was making us devious.

I know that censorship and blocking are frequently used devices by most parents but I personally never felt the need to do this to Laurie. Sex was something we talked about openly so she did not have a repressed interest in the topic. If she had wanted to visit websites of that type she would have found a way to do it whether or not we attempted to control it. Humans have a natural interest about things that are being censored from their lives and I chose not to turn that curiosity into something she would have to hide from me if that curiosity was present. When she was older she visited a few sexually oriented websites and quickly became bored. She told me that she went to these sites but because she did not have a need to hide it from me it was never an issue between us.

When you attempt to censor things out of a child's life you are fighting a losing battle. You may make the point about what offends you and set guidelines for your home but do not be fooled into thinking you are preventing the child from seeing or hearing what offends you. Vulgarity has become acceptable on the playgrounds, at school, in the movies and everywhere else we go. I am not saying that you must embrace the things that offend you. I am saying that a child is naturally curious about everything in life and if something is accepted everywhere but in the home his curiosity is piqued even further. The offense becomes something that grabs his attention to the point of distraction, and he "tries to get away with it" as often as possible. Accepting that these things go on in life and ignoring them makes them disappear from the child's mind faster. Making a huge fuss when children curse assures that they will curse every chance they get outside of the home. It is inevitable that a child will fight dictatorship by adults.

When Laurie was younger we would have limited the movies to PG movies but there was no need because she censored her own viewing until about age twelve. She was not impressed by violence, bad language or sex scenes. She often watched movies many times and knew when cursing would happen. She would put her fingers in her ears and hum because she had seen her dad do that when young children were visiting. I assume that he was unsure of what reaction to have when cursing happened around children as it made him uncomfortable.

As Laurie reached her teen years we prevented her from seeing movies with sex and violence in them. I was uncomfortable with the censorship but it was something that her dad was resolute about and I went along with it for the most part. In hindsight we should not have censored any books that she read or movies that she watched. I was unschooling Laurie to better prepare her for the real world and by censoring any aspect of that real world I was doing her a disservice. My parents censored so many things in their home that when my brothers and I were away from home we had a morbid fascination in seeing and hearing those censored things.

When Laurie was sixteen, she and I walked into a video store and she asked, "What does it feel like to be able to see any movie in here?" I knew that I had made an error in judgment by allowing the censorship and she was beginning to resent it. I removed the restrictions and my bond with Laurie became stronger and on a more mature level than it had been. How could I expect her to have an open mind if mine was partially closed?

Many of the things that are commonly restricted in homes are heard and seen almost everywhere else. We may have kept some cursing, sexual content and violence from her for a few years, but in the long run we did more harm than good. I took a bond of trust that Laurie had with me and put it in danger by trying to 'protect' her from something that was ultimately harmless. She was made unduly curious about a few television shows that would not have held her interest without the restriction. Shortly after the constraints were lifted she and I stopped watching television altogether. I have not watched for almost four years while she has recently started watching one or two shows a week. We occasionally rent a video and watch that, but the average trance-inducing television show can no longer hold our interest.

Laurie was introduced to computers at age ten by my sister Laura. She showed Laurie how to log on to other computers via modem through a phone line and connect with a local bulletin board system (BBS) much like we do today with the Internet. Once she was connected to the BBS she could chat with local users, play certain computer games with the other users, ask questions, give answers or simply post a message of her own choosing. Laurie was enamored of computers from the minute she sat down at one.

She had typed on an electric typewriter since she was a toddler so the keyboard was not a new experience.

By the following Christmas her father and I were aware that she needed a computer of her own. I was originally against having a computer in the house because I was interested in living a more self-sufficient lifestyle. All it took to change my mind was hearing the enthusiasm in Laurie's voice when she talked about computing. That Christmas morning she walked into the living room to see a new computer covered with a white sheet. Her eyes were huge as she pulled the sheet off to reveal her gift, and the rest of the day was spent setting the computer up in the spare bedroom and hooking the modem up so that she could get online. We became a two-phone-line household and soon wondered how we had ever gotten along without a computer in the house. Her typing speed rapidly increased to approximately seventy-five words a minute because of all of the hours spent at the keyboard.

Laurie immensely enjoyed her time spent online and she soon knew that she wanted to start her own BBS. This would mean that her computer would be tied up with BBS business most of the time because it should stay online for twenty-four hours a day so that users could connect to it at their convenience. She did some research to find out what was required to start the BBS that she decided to call "Dreams," and we purchased another computer. Once she had compiled all of the research and understood fully what she would need to do to get Dreams up and running she started working on it. This was done before Windows was efficient so she had to learn DOS, which is not as user-friendly. Her dad understood computer terminology but I was not as involved in the learning process and I was totally confused by many of their conversations. I had no idea at that time that computers would end up being so important to our family.

When Laurie started the installation of Dreams she became frustrated and put it aside for several months while she played with the new computer. She still had the desire to start Dreams though and eventually stayed up one night until the installation was complete. A friend that was the system operator (sysop) from another BBS helped her through much of the process via the telephone. Later the next day she came into the living room with a huge smile on her face announcing, "Dreams is ready." Laurie was now the only female sysop in southwest Louisiana at age sixteen. As one BBS after another shut down because of the popularity of the Internet, she became the sysop of the only operating BBS in the area.

During the first six months of Dreams the user list grew to close to one hundred users with about twenty regular users that phoned in every day. Laurie was dedicated to keeping Dreams running smoothly and tackled problems as soon as they arose. It was a time-consuming and demanding task but being at home allowed her to spend the time needed to keep it going. She eventually had a get-together for the users at a local pizza parlor where she met some of them face-to-face and made friendships that have lasted through the years. Two of her present-day closest friends, John M. and John S. were users of the BBS and became like part of our family.

John S. lived with us for a year and worked at a local computer store. He helped us purchase the components for two more computers which Laurie and her friends assembled. She became proficient at installing components and understanding the inside workings of a computer, and regularly saves maintenance costs by taking care of the computers herself.

Laurie's life centered on computers for approximately eight years. Her time online was not an issue and we did not monitor her use of the computer. At age eighteen when Laurie began working, her interest in the computer and the BBS began to wane. When she started college later that year the computer was gradually relegated to the task of research and assignments. It became a tool to use but she no longer enjoyed spending hours just being online. Her world had become larger than the Internet.

During the eight years that computers dominated Laurie's life, books were not as important to her and she at times felt guilty about that. She told me one time that she knew she would eventually return to reading but that right now she felt obsessed with the computer. I heard all of the negative comments about how computers take over our lives if we let them and do more harm than good. I was accustomed to Laurie's method of immersion-learning and did not worry that she would be harmed by spending so much time online. The computer is a complex tool and it takes time to learn how to use it.

Computers are in our futures. When a child spends hours on a computer she is not wasting her time even if she is 'only' playing computer games. She is becoming accomplished with a tool that will enrich her life and possibly lead to a career choice, as there are very few careers that do not require computer skills. If the lines of communication have been open between you she will not feel the need to sneak around the Internet and 'get into trouble.' Make it your business to know about the dangers online such as chatting, making purchases and hidden costs regarding sexually explicit websites. Talk openly about them with your child. Pretending that these dangers do not exist does not make them disappear. Keep yourself informed about what is going on when connected to the World Wide Web. Naivete and ignorance are what gets us into trouble.

Laurie got a Nintendo game system when she was eight years old and played whenever she had the desire, preferring the Mario games, Tetris and word games. When her cousin Asher came over they played Tecmo Baseball on the Nintendo for hours, sometimes playing half of the night. Laurie played Nintendo just like she did everything else – she immersed herself in learning a game, played it until she was tired of it, then left it for something else, occasionally picking it up again for a little while. I enjoyed watching her play some of the games and would sit on the bed with her and watch, cheering her on when she was doing well and gasping when the character 'died.'

Two years later Laurie got a computer and discovered a few strategy games that she enjoyed playing with no time limits set by us. I did not know exactly what she was getting from the games but I trusted that she would get what she needed from them then move on to something else. The time was not wasted because at the very least she gained computer skills and we had some great laughs when I attempted to play.

I have had many parents complain to me that their child spends too much time on the games. I suggest that they stop worrying about this and let the child 'burn out' on the games without it becoming an issue in the family. We all need a little mindless recreation time in our lives and children in school need more than the rest of us. Unwinding after a day sitting in class can help achieve some kind of balance in their mental state. If the parent can refrain from making it an issue the compulsion to play will pass. Your child is getting something from these games and she knows what she needs. Let her get that something and move on to other pursuits. It is highly unlikely that she will still be playing the games in five years with as much obsession as she is now. She will however, remember the respect that you showed her when she was a 'game-head.'

I played a few of the games myself to the point of obsession, especially Tetris. I have thought about why that game held my attention for so many hours at a time and I think I came up with a conclusion. There were times in my life that I could not seem to get things in order no matter how hard I tried. In Tetris the objective is to place falling blocks in a row across the screen, keeping up as the speed increases. Maybe I needed this game to occupy my mind and my hands temporarily in a way that gave me time to think in an organized fashion, or maybe I just needed to 'zone out' and be mindless for a while. I only know that I was obsessed with playing for a while, then I no longer wanted to play. No harm was done. I was not 'wasting my life' but simply needed the distraction.

Laurie's cousin Matt was so obsessed with video games that he spent every penny he got buying and renting games and every spare waking moment playing them. He was an honors student in high school and is now in a PhD program at a university in Utah. The hundreds of hours he spent in front of the television screen did not hurt his ability to pursue his interests. In fact they may have prompted his interest in graphic design.

How much television watching to allow seems to be the topic of conversation and much controversy in many homes. We were the average family watching sitcoms at night and I watched a few soap operas during the day when Laurie was a toddler. Laurie's dad told me that he thought letting Laurie watch soap operas was not a good idea. I basically ignored him thinking she was not really paying attention to them. One day three-year old Laurie corrected me during a conversation with a friend on what two characters on the show had said. I quit watching them that day.

Laurie watched Sesame Street for about a year then became bored with the monotony. She watched Calliope, a collection of fairy tales and cartoons, for a period of time also. We did not control her television viewing hours and let her watch as much as she wanted to watch. Some days she would watch television for three to four hours and other days she would not turn it on at all. She preferred reading, writing or playing in her room. At age twenty-two she now watches television for approximately two hours a week with a group of friends. She will rent movies from time-to-time but finds that her life is too busy for the typical television show. As an eighteen-year old she watched MTV sporadically but soon became bored with that.

I am aware of the arguments against children watching too much television. Their lives become sedentary and some of the garbage on television is not fit for anyone to watch. So much time is 'wasted' in front of the boob-tube. I am not an advocate for or against television. I personally do not watch it and have not for four years except on rare occasions. This was my decision after forty-two years of viewing. I was one of the kids that watched television every evening when I got home from school. I now know that it was an escape from the school day that helped me unwind.

I approached Laurie's television viewing just as I did everything else. She controlled how much time to spend in front of the television. Some children can watch television endlessly but Laurie was inclined to turn it off after a short while. All children are different and need different amounts of escapes and distractions. I think that not making television watching an issue helped Laurie walk away from it easier. She knew she could turn it on at any time so she did not try to cram in extra viewing whenever she could.

Peer Pressure

"True it is that she who escapeth safe and unpolluted from out the school of freedom, giveth more confidence of herself than she who cometh sound out of the school of severity and restraint."

~Michel Eyquem De Montaigne~

If I had to choose what I thought was the single most harmful aspect of going to school I would have to say peer pressure. Hardly anyone has the inner strength to combat the pressure to conform; especially when someone she admires or even idolizes is putting on the pressure. Her determination to do what she feels is right is weakened by the need to fit in. The majority of us want to feel like we are part of a group rather than being an outsider but for a child the need is much stronger. If her opinions are not yet fully formed or she is rebelling against something in her life, she may begin imitating someone that she feels is tough and independent. She might become a follower in a 'bad crowd' and end up in trouble that she cannot handle and did not expect. Appearing tough becomes even more important to her and she will take chances to insure her reputation.

I have talked to adult friends about their experiences with peer pressure. I was surprised to find out that the people I thought were the 'strong' ones in school, the ones that set the

171

standards for the rest of us, were under even more pressure than I was. Because of their reputation for setting those standards they were constantly trying to stay ahead of the game by knowing what was supposed to be 'cool.' The strong ones were in a race with each other most of the time. They wanted to maintain their lead so figuring out what they should wear or what phrases they should incorporate into their speech was imperative. In addition to this they told me that the reason they felt the need to be the style setters was because they were being pressured at home to be leaders.

Peer pressure was something we seldom encountered in our home. Maybe Laurie's self-confidence was due to a lack of pressure by other children to conform. When other children were at our home Laurie was the leader. They wanted to have Laurie's life and looked at her as the 'cool' one. On the rare occasion that they tried to convince her to do something she was against, she quickly told them "No," because the other kids' opinions never seemed to bother her. She marched to the beat of her own drum and had no fear of speaking her mind.

When she was in her late teens she went to a bookstore with one of her best friends. They were looking at computer books and one book had a CD inside the front cover. Her friend winked at her and said he was going to take the CD. She quickly chastised him and told him that he was not going to steal while she was with him and that if he needed the CD that badly she would buy it for him. They are still best of friends after five years, and he told me that Laurie was the most honest person he had ever known and that he respected her highly.

The peer pressure that I hear the most about concerns drinking, drugs and designer clothing. Laurie went through a Nike phase when she was fifteen, then made the decision that paying extra to advertise a brand name was ridiculous, and she became an advocate against shoes, clothing and accessories with name brands on them. She now buys her clothing in second-hand shops (Goodwill is her favorite) and still refuses to buy some designer clothes even at much-reduced prices.

The pressure to wear certain clothing is more than just a financial issue in most homes. It becomes an issue that causes a rift between parents and the children. The children want so desperately to fit in and not having the 'right' clothes makes them feel inferior. When their parents refuse to spend the extra money for the 'right' clothing, the children think that the parents are insensitive to something that will embarrass them daily in school. The parents think the kids are out of their minds wanting them to spend that kind of money on clothing. I am so glad that this was not an issue in our home. To be honest, I am not sure how I would have handled it. I would hate Laurie to feel inferior, but I would also hate for her to be so shallow as to think her clothing made that much difference with true friends.

Peer pressure causes a child to conform to the beliefs and actions of others. It gives him something to believe in, which is why street gangs are so popular. If a child's belief system is intact before setting out into the world it is much easier for him to stick to his beliefs. If he understands his beliefs he can recognize if they need to be modified. Laurie knows she is different and that she stands out in a crowd and she wears this knowledge with pride. Being different would have devastated my ego when I was younger. Laurie's happiness and her inner strength are the two things that give me the most appreciation that unschooling was the right thing to do.

Sex and Dating

"The human heart, at whatever age, opens only to the heart that opens in return."

~Maria Edgeworth~

I hesitated about whether or not to discuss sex because of the discomfort that the word causes some adults when faced with the thought of talking to their children. I then realized that this is precisely the reason I must address the topic. As adults we are fully aware that sex is a natural part of our existence, but for a myriad of reasons sex has been turned into something that is anything but natural in the minds of many people. Media is the easiest scapegoat and the one most commonly blamed for the blatant degradation of sex. I agree that media has made sex into some kind of otherworldly topic. There is so much information available on the World Wide Web that we are confused and unsure of what is 'normal' and what is perverse. The media is not totally to blame however. We think that if we do not mention sex to our children that they will magically know what is acceptable to us and never cross that line between what we perceive as right and wrong. If we do not tell them where that line is and why we feel the way we do then how do we expect them to know?

I was never given "the talk." I might be mistaken but I have no memory of my parents ever saying the word "sex" to me. I think they assumed that if they did not tell me about sex that I would not have sex or hormonal feelings. I was so ignorant that I did not even know what to ask them much less how to ask them anything pertaining to sex. I also felt that they were unapproachable on the subject and that I would be forbidden to ask any questions on the topic because we were reprimanded if we mentioned anything sexual. I am not saying this to degrade their parenting skills but to say that the majority of my peers were treated the same way. Talk of sex, not to mention the act itself, was taboo.

I pretended to know what was going on when I was with my peers even though I was clueless. When Laurie was born I vowed to make sex a natural topic. I did not click television shows off when they were showing animals procreating nor did I gasp and feign shame when sex was mentioned on television or in real life. When Laurie was two years old she became curious about her body and started asking questions and I answered with sincere honesty and no embarrassment or shame.

Laurie and her male cousin noticed their differences when she was two and he was four while bathing together. They looked, touched, said, "Hmmm…" then went back to playing with the toys in the bathtub. I watched but did not react knowing that it never occurred to them that they had done anything "dirty" or "immoral."

That was innocence at its best. Several months passed before Laurie asked me why her cousin was 'different.' At age two I saw no reason to fill her in on all of the details about sex but I did tell her about the differences between boys and girls discussing the fact that boys had a penis and girls had a vagina. She was interested but not prepared to ask many questions, so I only answered the questions she asked and did not elaborate. She was satisfied and went back to playing.

From time-to-time she would ask questions seemingly out of the blue. Maybe she had heard someone say something or she had seen something in a book or on television. I am not always sure where the thoughts came from but I made it a point to answer honestly and not make up something that was 'easier' for me to say.

By the time she was a teenager with more involved questions requiring lengthier answers from me, there was no embarrassment or worry for either of us. She knew that ultimately, sex was something beautiful between two people that loved each other. There were no prejudices, no fears and no misunderstandings in what she knew. I was careful not to put my moral standards as a rule for her to live by because I wanted her to be her own person in control of her own body. Laurie and I can discuss anything including sex, with candor. When you approve of your child you can talk to them about anything and everything. Approval makes many inhibitions disappear.

Sex is not some dirty little secret to laugh and giggle about or shame children about. It is a facet of our lives that needs to be addressed. Talking about sex openly with your child assures that he will not go into his dating years with no legitimate information on the subject. In light of the AIDS epidemic you are risking your child's life if you are not open and honest with him. It also will not be something that he participates in as an act of rebellion against his uptight parents if he has all the facts. There are many books that will help you talk to your child about sex.

Dating was a bittersweet experience for most of us. I was elated that boys were asking me out on most weekends during high school but filled with dread about how to conduct myself on these dates. Being asked on numerous dates was a self-esteem boost but the actual dates lowered my self-confidence. I wanted to be popular with the boys and knew that the line must be drawn somewhere. I did not realize just how far a boy would go to achieve his 'goal.' I dated boys who were well known to be of high morals and good ethics and were popular in high school. I assumed that they did not become octopi on dates but I was bitterly disappointed with almost all of them. Trying to fight them off without appearing too uptight became the main event of each date and when they discovered that I was not 'easy' they did not ask me out again. If I had been less naive about what was going on in most boys' minds my dating life would have been more pleasurable. I would not have worried about their approval nor been disappointed when they did not ask me out again.

I feel certain that this happened to more girls than just me but I did not talk about what had happened. Obviously no one did. There was a feeling of guilt that accompanied these dates. I thought surely that I must have done something to make them think I was "easy" although I did not know what. I learned through my own experiences and feel fortunate that none of them forced themselves on me. The guilt that often stays with a woman when she has been raped is easy for me to understand in light of the guilt that I felt after these dates.

I did not want Laurie to go into dating with no knowledge or discussion of what might happen. I did not want to scare her and make her think that dating was a nightmare, but keeping her ignorant would be negligence on my part. I handled it as diplomatically and as honestly as I could. I must have done well because Laurie is always in control when she is on a date and has no qualms about drawing the line whether or not she is 'liked' by her date.

When Laurie was a child I was fond of saying, "When she is thirty-five years old she can start dating, but only double-dating." I said this in jest but was not anxious for her dating age to approach. On her seventeenth birthday she was still not interested in dating and her dad and I breathed a sigh of relief. But alas, several months later she went on her first date.

By then I had changed my attitude and was even a bit excited that she was about to embark on another facet of growing up. I knew that she was a responsible person and I had faith in her ability to control any situation that might arise. We had always talked openly and honestly about all issues, including sex, and I said everything to her that I wished my parents had said to me as a teenager. She was well informed about hormonal feelings and how easily things could get out of control. Laurie and John M. dated exclusively for almost three years. They no longer date but are still close friends, always there for each other when needed. Their friendly relationship is a result of intricate communication between each other and with me. They often came to me with questions and received honest answers.

When your child acts as if she knows it all about boys and dating she is only protecting her pride. If you have not talked openly throughout her life then it is almost impossible for her to approach you at this awkward time. If honest talk begins at an early age then it is much easier as the child matures. Not talking openly to her about boys, dating and sex puts her self-esteem level in danger, not to mention her life. This is not a time to let embarrassment stand in the way of open communication. Your child matures rapidly and these issues are on her mind twenty-four hours a day; to ignore this fact is irresponsible. Do not mince words or assume that she probably knows something. Say it all and say it with compassion and understanding, not with an attitude of, "You better not do so-and-so." Sexual feelings are inevitable in the teen years and she must know the consequences of acting upon those feelings and realize the situations that are possible with dating. Both boys and girls should have confidence in themselves to stop any advances made by the other person. Without that confidence a fear takes over that is so overwhelming as to leave the child defenseless against an aggressive date.

There's no room for hinting and moralizing in this day and age of so many STDs, including HIV/AIDS. There's no room for power-tripping authoritarian parenting in the confusing life of teens. They need love, respect and sincere acceptance of who they are or they will find it in the arms of another teen who is also in need of the same thing. Tough love, repression and strict parenting push the kids to find approval elsewhere. Very few teens escape this accepted way of parenting unscathed.

Drugs and Alcohol

"A man must consider what a rich realm he abdicates when he becomes a conformist."

~Ralph Waldo Emerson~

Drugs and alcohol are tough subjects to approach when talking to your children so it is very important that you keep the subject open for discussion in your home. I grew up in the sixties, a generation known for accepting drugs and alcohol with open arms, but I also grew up in a home where neither was used or discussed. I was amazed when I discovered that the majority of my peers' parents drank socially. I thought alcohol was an evil thing not to be mentioned much less partaken of. I was repeatedly in the home of 'drinkers' who were good parents and who treated me with respect. My parents were even friends with some of them so this was confusing for me.

I was in awe of a beer or mixed drink and it fascinated me to think that so many people drank this "evil" liquid while we were not to even mention the vile stuff in our home. I was 'repressed.' I had so many questions and no one to ask without risking condemnation at home or embarrassment by my more knowledgeable peers. How could something so many nice people enjoyed be so evil?

As I got older I came to the conclusion that my parents were pushing their beliefs down my throat and I rebelled. I married, left home at age eighteen and began drinking far too much to compensate for my innocence. I wanted so desperately to be accepted by my peers. Beer was my drink of choice, not because I loved the taste but because it seemed like the way to best show my independence from my uptight family. I realized over twenty years ago that I did not even like the taste of beer. I vowed to do whatever it took to keep Laurie from being a rebellious drinker.

Laurie grew up knowing that some people drink and some do not. She learned that there was nothing wrong with having a social drink as long as the drinking was not out of control, and people who enjoy social drinking are not necessarily 'bad' people because they drink.

I knew from experience that peer pressure to drink or take drugs was present in many situations. When Laurie was around age seventeen I told her that I understood the pressures of her age about drugs and drinking and that if there was anything she wanted to try to please try it at home where it was safe and I could be there with her. I knew Laurie well and felt that she would not want to try anything but I also remembered the pressures from other teens. Her reply was, "Mom those are things that people use for escapes and I have nothing to escape from." Some parents are oblivious to the fact that schooled children are often pressured to try sex, drugs and alcohol as early as the first

184

grade. The knowledge that we had raised a child in such a way that she did not feel the need for 'escapes' will always be one of my most self-satisfying achievements.

The relief that I felt when Laurie said that she had nothing to escape from did not come only from the knowledge that she was not feeling pressure to try drugs or alcohol but from the feeling of being validated about the way we had raised her. "I have nothing to escape from." What those words meant to me was, "You have been such great parents that I am satisfied with my life. You have given me love and respect and everything that I needed. I love things the way they are and would not change a thing." She was not saying that as a ploy to attain favor or a materialistic gift. It was straight from her heart and her logical mind. Why take a substance to alter reality when you are satisfied with your reality?

She did not want to cling to her parents and hide from the world nor was she taking this stance because she was afraid. She was not a 'goody-two-shoes' with a squeaky clean reputation to protect. She simply did not need the escape. This conversation with her put our unschooling lifestyle into a nutshell for me. We had given her a sense of well being that most people lack. Even teenagers who seem to have the perfect home life want to get away from it as a way to feel their independence. The non-coercive parenting and unschooling were instrumental to Laurie feeling independent throughout her childhood with no tension making her want to escape from her home.

Driving

The ability to drive gives a teen independence and a feeling of maturity. It is difficult to watch our children leave home behind the wheel of a car but it is going to happen in most cases. He usually obtains a driving permit first so that he can drive with one adult in the car and no other passengers, giving him practice before he sets out on his own. It is difficult to not backseat-drive when your child is driving but he is nervous enough without his parents' comments. Waiting for him to ask a question is the best way to handle that unless he is doing something dangerous. In that case, point it out as calmly as possible.

A child learns proper defensive driving by watching his parents drive. If they stay calm and drive carefully he will most likely drive the same way. There are many offensive drivers on the road and it is impossible for a new driver to know how to handle all situations involving the aggressive driver. If you point out the aggressive drivers for several years before your child gets his license and let him see how you handle the situation he will be more prepared to react properly when he is confronted with the same predicament.

When your child is driving and has to deal with a hostile driver, try to calmly instruct them on what to do. This is a tricky time for a child learning to drive because he does not want to be told what to do. He is most likely terrified of the other driver and not sure what he should do. You will know what your child needs from you if you are watching, listening and remembering how you felt when you were learning to drive.

When Laurie reached driving age, fifteen in Louisiana, she was not that anxious to get her driver's license even after taking the drivers' education course. I was able to take her to the places she wanted to go and staying home was more conducive for her to do the things that interested her. I contrasted her attitude about driving with mine when I was her age. I wanted to drive all of the time and I would volunteer to go to the store for Mom every day. The idea of driving was thrilling to me. The seriousness of being behind the wheel never entered my conscious mind and I was quite reckless at times.

Laurie's aunt had been killed a few years earlier in an automobile accident so Laurie was painfully aware of the dangers on the road. She got her license at age sixteen but was not anxious to drive until she got a job working at a video store at age eighteen. We had a car and a manual transmission truck and she learned to drive them both. The truck was difficult to drive and neither of us truly enjoyed expending the strength that it took to handle the shifting and steering. Her dad thought it was important that she know how to drive a manual transmission and we are all glad that she can drive one if she needs to.

When Laurie started college we bought her a small car for traveling the thirty-mile round trip each day. She became more familiar with driving and less timid with each trip she made. She now lives in a larger city and does fine. She has mentioned to me that driving is still not her favorite thing to do but that she does not let that stop her from going places.

Homework

"Have you done your homework?" Oh, how I hated to hear that every night when I was younger. I knew when I had homework and I knew that I had to do the homework but I was not trusted to take care of it without a reminder. I know that my parents felt that it was their responsibility to ask that question because 'good' parents would see to it that their child's homework is done. Getting homework done puts pressure on the child, the parents and the relationship between them. I knew that doing my homework was necessary to maintain my high grades and keep my parents and teachers happy but it brought me to the heights of frustration. If I understood what was taught in class then the work was redundant and time-consuming. If I had not understood working on it alone at night was fruitless. Either way it was boring and repetitious and I would much rather have been reading a book of my own choosing.

One of the things that the parents of school children are asked to do to help them accelerate in school is to make sure that they do their homework. On the surface it makes sense that if a child spends time at home working the same types of problems that he learned in school that day the concept will sink in and she will be better able to figure it out for tests. No one considers that she has already spent seven hours of her day sitting in a classroom learning things that bore her to death and she certainly does not want to spend her evening going over the same things again. The parents have also spent the day working, and time in the evening should involve pleasurable experiences between parents and their children, not verbose and boring schoolwork.

I remember sitting around the dining table with my brothers while we did our homework every evening. I do not remember any of the actual assignments but I do recall the feelings while doing the work – resentment at the teacher for assigning it. The favorite teachers among students were the ones that did not give homework assignments. The ease of the class was the deciding issue regardless of whether we enjoyed the class or not. We just wanted to get a passing grade and go home for the summer. In middle school my history teacher was the favorite among students because of his impertinence toward his peers and the countenance expected of teachers. The girls had to stay in the back of the room and visit while the boys went up to his desk to hear him tell jokes several days a week. He not only never assigned homework, but the infrequent tests were incredibly easy. He seemed to hold every aspect of teaching in contempt and later quit teaching to become a realtor.

As a college student I found out that long hours of homework and research were necessary because there was more to learn than a professor could teach in class. Laurie had never done homework before college but she regularly did it on time and had no problems adjusting from a life without homework to a life with it. Doing busywork for twelve years prior to college would not have helped her acclimate to the work that she needed to do at the university. Instead it would have attached a negative connotation to the task that she now enjoys.

During our first semester she felt that I had been on the Internet too long one evening and she walked into my room with her hands on her hips demanding, "Have you done your homework yet, Mom?" She was totally serious but I could not help but see the irony because it had never been necessary for me to ask her that and here she was interrogating me for an answer. I replied sheepishly that I had not done my homework and she chastised me and went back to her own homework remarking, "I just don't want you to embarrass me in class." That is one of my favorite memories of college because of the humor and because it was obvious proof that she took college seriously.

Measures of Intelligence

Tests and Grades

"I believe that the testing of the student's achievements in order to see if he meets some criterion held by the teacher, is directly contrary to the implications of therapy for significant learning."

~Carl Rogers~

Some of us panic when we are faced with a test. Our hands get clammy, our pulse quickens and the information needed to pass the test is whirling around in our heads in chaotic confusion or not there at all. It does not matter that we studied for hours the night before the test and knew all of the information. The mere thought of the test makes us feel afraid and stupid. It is that conviction that causes us to lose grasp of the responses to the questions.

There are as many ways to give a test as there are test-givers. Some teachers want the students to do well and they give excellent notes and reviews. Some tests seem alien and devoid of anything that was taught in class. Deciphering what each test-giver wants is half of the battle. One might be happy with one-word answers while another one wants an essay. Many teachers seem to take perverse pleasure in tricking you into marking an incorrect answer. At other times tests seem so easy that you worry needlessly that you must have gotten confused.

In one of the classes that Laurie and I were taking, the professor would give a review of what topics were going to be on the test. Each test would cover numerous pages of notes and over one hundred pages in the textbook. To pose a question she would take a sentence from the book and alter it slightly. If I used common sense to answer the question I could be wrong. She seemed to have a knack for finding the most confusing way to word a question, and delight at the low marks some of the students received. Helping students learn was not her intent but seeing how many she could fail.

Laurie's first test ever was for her drivers' license and her second test was the ACT to enter college. I was with her every day of her life so I knew what she knew and what she did not know and it seemed silly to test her knowledge. In Louisiana you could request that your child be tested annually, but I never saw the reasoning behind doing that with a child raised in freedom. When she was six years old should I have given her a test for first graders? What about when she was seven? She was reading at an adult level by then but her math skills were low. At age fifteen she would not have done well on a fourth grade math test. This did not mean that she was a failure but that she had not reached a point in life when math was important to her.

When children initiate their own learning, it does not follow a curriculum designed by authorities deeming what they should know at a certain age. What would have been the result of testing Laurie? Would the high scores in some subjects have made her feel good enough about herself to wipe out the feeling of failure with the low score in math? Would the low score in math affect her high scores in college algebra and statistics? Grades served no purpose in her life because she was doing her best indifferent to any measuring system instilled by school authorities. When learning is fun and constant there is no need to test.

My beliefs concerning grades are equal to my opinions of testing. The grades are an accumulation of test scores, homework scores, class participation and the individual teacher's judgment. Grades tend to put students into one of three categories: intelligent, average or stupid, and there are negative aspects associated with each category. If you are initially labeled in the 'intelligent' category you are expected to live up to that throughout your education. If you relax and let your grades drop then you hear, "I know you can do better than that. You just have to apply yourself more." The 'average' category is probably the safest one to be in because no one expects you to achieve 'intelligent' status. You are still expected not to fall to 'stupid' status. Most children learn just how much work is necessary to stay in the average zone. Laurie told me that she figured out in college just what she had to do to make an A and put forth no further effort except in classes that she genuinely loved.

The 'average' classification sometimes follows a child into adulthood although some manage to escape that stereotype and become happy and successful. If you fall into the 'stupid' classification early on the stigma is usually devastating. You feel that you need not apply yourself to schoolwork at all and that generally carries over into other aspects of your life. If you accept this categorization of 'stupid' and believe it your character will need to be strong to leave this disgrace behind you. Being a child is hard enough without having to prove your intelligence in the light of bad grades.

For students who are terrified by negative reactions at home to their low grades testing creates a moral dilemma at times. They know that cheating is 'wrong' and that getting caught at cheating would be worse than receiving a low mark on a test. Do they take a chance at getting caught in hopes that they will receive a higher mark on their test or do they accept the consequences of the low grade and refuse to cheat? The fear of their parents' reaction is sometimes in itself enough apprehension to make them score lower on the test.

What motive do grades serve in our society if not to put us in a specific classification? I was in the 'intelligent' category in school yet it took me many years to overcome the anxiety involved in growing up and feel that I was possessed of any intellect whatsoever. It was also difficult dealing with the 'failure' perceived by others when I as an intelligent person, made the decision to be a stay-at-home mother and later a writer, rather than a college graduate. Being a mother is not all that I thought I was capable of doing. It is all that I truly wanted to do. Why was I measured by a scale of acceptance that means nothing to me? Why is anyone? Some of the most personally satisfied and financially successful people that I know never attended college or had any desire to further their education.

When I decided to attend college at age forty-three I did not have a career choice in mind. I was allowing society's idea of success, a college degree, to insinuate itself into my destiny. Was the outcome a positive one? In my opinion the outcome was positive because I realized that a college degree was not what I needed to feel successful. To be fair, it was the classes requiring essays that made me see how much I enjoyed writing. However, my decision to drop out of college was not perceived as a positive move by some. According to them I made high grades in college and I could easily instill myself in an occupation that would befit an 'intelligent' person, disregarding the fact that I had no interest in those occupations. It seemed ridiculous to work so hard for four years with the objective being something I was not interested in. I did not want a career just for financial security; happiness and contentment with what I am doing is more important to me. I would rather live with a smaller paycheck than dread going to work each morning.

I have thought about the high grades I made in college and the effort that it took to make those grades. During the first few semesters my mind was set on earning a degree and making the high marks seemed more important, although many students earn a degree while making barely passing grades. I spent hours studying subjects that bored me to the point of distraction so that I could 'prove' my intelligence. I realized that I was not making A's because I enjoyed learning like Laurie did, but because I was worried about others' perceptions of my aptitude. The last few 'serious' semesters had me in a quandary since I realized I no longer wanted a degree but wanted to pursue my writing. I slacked off on my obsession with A's and allowed myself the luxury of making a few B's before dropping out, knowing that my parents and Laurie's dad would be disappointed in me. However, I could no longer ignore my yearning to write.

When I realized that spending time with Laurie in school was my true motive for being there I attended one final semester, taking her senior-level classes with her. I thoroughly enjoyed those months with her and effortlessly made all A's because I finally had my mind settled on what I was going to do; I was going to write. Raising Laurie and writing are two of the things I have been most passionate about in my life and tests and grades did nothing to assist me in these endeavors. If anything the ill effects from them had to be overcome so that I could succeed. Loving what you are doing is the true measure of success, not a system of grades, judgments and guidelines set up by others. The younger we are when that is instilled in our mind, the easier it will be for us to find our purpose in life.

IQ

"If the aborigine drafted an IQ test, all of Western civilization would presumably flunk it."

~Stanley Garn~

Often when I tell others about unschooling and how it impacted Laurie's life they reply, "But she's intelligent. It wouldn't work with my kid." It is true that Laurie has an above average Intelligence Quotient according to a simple test that she took online, but I do not credit her high IQ for all of her success. I do feel that the way she was raised may have given her a few extra points on her IQ score. There are tests being conducted to prove that it is possible to elevate your IQ. Any child that is given the opportunities that Laurie was given will have a higher self-confidence level and that will result in higher learning ability.

Laurie's IQ may make it easier for her to pursue an academic career but that is not my definition of success. The fact that she loves academics and is living her life pursuing them is the important thing. If she were maintaining a 4.0 in college and not enjoying herself she would quit and find her passion in life. I feel that the unschooling lifestyle insures that she will always follow her heart and do what makes her happy. It is all that she knows.

Your IQ has little to do with your success in life. If you do not have a high level of self-esteem and you feel insecure with who you are, your full potential cannot be reached. It has long been common knowledge that emotional intelligence (EQ) is a greater predictor of success. This has nothing to do with your IQ level; it has more to do with your personality and attitude toward life. Believing in yourself and your child does not require genius. It requires love, trust, respect and faith.

College

"We learn simply by the exposure of living. Much that passes for education is not education at all but ritual. The fact is that we are being educated when we know it least."

~David P. Gardner~

When Laurie was employed by a local video store she decided that working for minimum wage was not something she wanted to do any longer than she had to. Since she did not have a career choice in mind she decided at age eighteen to attend college. This was a major decision for someone who had never read a textbook or taken a test. I had silently hoped for several years that she would decide to attend college. I would have been supportive of any choice she made but I still held onto the belief that a college graduate is more successful and better prepared for the future than a non-graduate is. I believed like society, that a college degree defined success. I have since changed my opinion but I am thankful that Laurie made the college choice because she loves it.

We picked up a catalog from the local university and she read it from cover to cover. Her two friends, John M. and John S. decided that they were also going so there were catalogs left on the tables at all times. I picked a catalog up one evening when the kids were working on the computers. I had attended college when I was eighteen and dropped out two weeks later because I hated it. However, things look different when you are forty-three years old. I walked into the room and asked the group, "Do you think I could handle college too?" They laughed at first thinking I was making a joke then saw that I was serious. Laurie was the first to say, "Of course you could Mom. Are you considering it?" I said that I was and they expressed their surprise and joy that I might be attending with them. I left the room and studied the catalog a little longer trying to choose a major that would interest me. I wondered about Nursing and went into the room and asked their opinion, "Do you think I'd be a good nurse?" They screamed, "NOOOOO!" We laughed and I decided on the neutrality of a Basic Studies course.

That week we went to the college to register and the admissions clerk told us that Laurie would need an equivalency diploma (GED) and that she would have to take the standard admission test (ACT). We felt that Laurie could do fine on every subject but math so she decided to go to 'night school' to learn math before taking the GED test. The class was a joke. Teachers sat at a table at the front of the room while the students brought their own workbooks and pencils and sat down and worked. If they had a question they could go forward and ask. This method of 'teaching' made Laurie feel so ignorant. She did not need help with a certain aspect of math, she needed to be taught math from the beginning. Her mind would wander and she would write poetry depicting herself as ignorant.

She voiced her disgust at home and her dad said, "If you aren't getting anything out of this then quit. You don't need this." She never returned. One of my friends who was a retired college professor informed us that the GED was not necessary to attend college, so we signed Laurie up to take the ACT, bypassing the registrar's office at the college. Laurie and John S. went to the testing center together and spent the day taking tests. When we received the results several weeks later we were amazed to find that she had scored a 25. She was admitted and we both registered.

I was a bit nervous when we attended Orientation. Here we were in an auditorium full of people (mostly teens) about to embark on an adventure that would change our lives. Tickets were handed out at the door and five lucky people would win door prizes. Laurie's ticket number was called and she went forward to the stage. The student emcee was clowning around trying to ease the tension in the auditorium but Laurie did not seem the least bit nervous. He asked her a few questions the first of which was, "Where did you go to school?" She said, "Nowhere. I was unschooled." He said, "Oh, homeschooled?" She said, "No unschooled. I was not taught anything." Laughter went through the auditorium and the young man said, "Who taught you?" She just gave him a deadpan look and said, "No one taught me. Unschooling is an unorthodox form of homeschooling where the kid learns whatever he or she is interested in." He was speechless and everyone laughed. After he regained his composure he asked her if she would like to say hello to anyone in the audience.

She grinned wickedly and said, "Yeah, my mom is attending college too. Hi Mom!" So much for me blending into the woodwork. I now had five hundred students looking at me while the emcee said, "Stand up Mom and wave to us!" I stood and he started asking me questions. He asked me when I graduated from high school and I said, "1973." Someone in the audience said, "Wow! That's before I was born." The emcee then said slightly under his breath, "That's before most of us were born!" Our induction into college life was one of laughter.

Laurie and I had several classes together throughout the years but I could not keep up with her rigid schedule. Some semesters she would take the maximum load of twenty-one hours (seven classes) while working full-time at a bookstore. She thrived on the work and never let her grades drop. Professors enjoyed her company and often asked her to help them with their personal computer problems. She became a teaching assistant to one of her favorite sociology professors, which meant that on certain hours each week she would be available to assist students with any questions they had.

She shared the office with the professor and the professor became a dear friend to both of us.

Being able to attend classes with Laurie was an incredible blessing for me. To sit in a class and watch your daughter absorb information, answer questions and take tests with ease was sheer delight. When students discovered that we were mother and daughter they would not hide their surprise when they found out that Laurie not only did not mind me being in her classes but she enjoyed it. I was a bit of a class clown at times while Laurie was a serious student.

Laurie's thought processes work differently from the majority of people. She approaches problems with logic that baffles me at times. I have been called 'practical' most of my life but her practicality far surpasses mine. Her reality is based on something that most of us seem to have lost during our school years. She sees things as they really are rather than from a schooled point of view. Our learning was based on the needs of the teachers, adults and peers in our lives; Laurie's learning was based on her own needs. There have been times when I struggled for the answer to a problem for hours. She would walk into the room and I would explain the problem to her, usually showing my frustration at my inability to figure it out. She would concentrate for a few minutes then solve the problem for me.

When Laurie replies to a question she answers holistically and logically leaving emotion out of the equation. She is in touch with her own personal feelings and does not apologize for them or qualify them to anyone. This may seem average for many people but for me it is very special and important. I was always a people-pleaser and have learned by watching Laurie that being true to myself is the only way to live a life free of inner turmoil.

Some people tell me that Laurie would probably have enjoyed school as a child since she enjoys college so much but I disagree. I think that one of the reasons she enjoys college so much is because she was not turned off of learning as a child. College was something that she chose to do. It was not something that strangers decided was mandatory for her life. She attends classes every day with renewed interest in the subjects and the desire to learn. There is very little redundancy in college compared to grade school, and this keeps her interested.

College and academics are not the only measure of success in life. There are many paths that lead to contentment and a real happiness with what you are doing. I am proud of Laurie and her achievements but I would be equally proud of her no matter what she chose to do as long as she is contented with her choice.

I have not kept in touch with any homeschooling/unschooling newsletters for the past fifteen years. I preferred to go with my instincts on our day-to-day lives. After I had written a large portion of this book I joined an online unschooling network and told them about Laurie, her college experiences and this book. I had forgotten that college is not the goal of the majority of unschoolers. It was not our goal either. Laurie's happiness was always foremost but college just happened to be what fulfilled her. I was put in a position to defend her choice to attend college and my pride in her high grades so I spent many hours considering the negativity surrounding college.

On the surface was the realization that I was proud of Laurie's 4.0 because it was a way for me to say to my family and society that my choosing to unschool Laurie was the right decision. Her high grades proved to the skeptics that she was not 'stupid' as a result of being unschooled, giving me a prideful attitude of "I was right and you were wrong." Looking deeper I know that my contentment with the way Laurie's life is going is because she is genuinely happy with what she is doing. I have the self-satisfaction of knowing that raising her the way I did, with self-regulation, means that she will never settle for something that does not befit her. She will not end up doing work that she does not love and that gives me peace of mind as a mother.

The majority of society believes that success can only be achieved through a college degree or having a job that commands a large salary. We have been conditioned from early childhood to believe that we must be docile and obedient so that we can work in jobs that offer no stimulation to the senses. When I was in high school I worked in an office typing addresses on envelopes for four hours a day. The job was so monotonous that I felt like screaming every evening when the office closed. I understood how a caged animal must feel with the only difference being that I had chosen to be there. I only stayed at this job for a few months but I can imagine the stress levels of people that stay with jobs that they do not enjoy.

A college degree does not make a person wise to the ways of the world. Laurie seems wiser about many issues than many middle-aged professionals who happen to be college graduates. Have their lives been so narrowed by their professional lives that they have ceased to participate in a life outside of their careers? Could it be that what they were taught and how they learned affected them negatively? In Gloria Steinem's book *Revolution From Within* is a chapter entitled, "The Importance of Un-learning," which states: "Once we are old enough to have had an education, the first step toward self-esteem for most of us is not to learn but to unlearn. We need to demystify the forces that have told us what we should be before we can value what we are." Ms. Steinem reports on the data that shows that as a woman's level of education rises her self-esteem level plummets. That was the answer I was searching for. Laurie has been finding out who she really was since she was a toddler because no one was dictating to her to be something that she was not. She did not have to overcome a low self-esteem.

Ms. Steinem writes about the patriarchal influence in college and how it affects the students. She mentions the personality traits seen as inherent in females that hold women back: self-sacrifice, a lack of personal will, living through others, fear of confrontation and a need for approval. This paragraph made me realize why Laurie enjoys college more than her fellow students. She has none of these traits. As a forty-three year old college student, I witnessed the timidity of the other students both male and female every day. They appeared terrified to speak up or take a stand about any of the issues. I remembered feeling this way myself when I attended college at age eighteen. On the other hand Laurie speaks out with confidence on any and all issues about which she has a conviction. She critiques the lectures of the professors knowing that their personal opinions are included in their words. She does not take their words to heart and seems to subconsciously weed out the extraneous information grasping what is valid and listening logically to what is being said. Most of the other students do not seem to have the comprehension to separate the facts from the professor's conception.

Does this observation mean that all unschoolers would do better in college than a previously schooled student? Would the gender of an unschooler make a difference in college? Perhaps the self-confidence that comes with being self-regulated all of your life gives you a head start in all endeavors, not just college. Being able to think for yourself and not just follow what others are doing cannot help but give you a different and more enlightened perspective on any topic.

All of these realizations made me aware of why college is so different for Laurie than it is for the other students. Her approach to life, including learning, is an optimistic one. College does not denigrate her because her self-confidence and high self-esteem cannot be affected by knowledge that is portrayed by a patriarchal and narrow-minded perspective of a professor. With the framework of her childhood behind her, college is a positive experience and I venture to say that the rest of her life will follow suit.

Socialization

"I am now quite cured of seeking pleasure in society, be it country or town. A sensible man ought to find sufficient company in himself."

~Emily Bronte~

One of the main concerns of most people when they learned that we were unschooling was the lack of socialization in Laurie's life. They felt that school was the only way in which social skills could be learned. I find it interesting that even though most adults experienced the antisocial reality of school, they still think of it as a social experience. No talking is allowed in most classrooms and breaks are usually a time to run to the restroom or eat lunch. The camaraderie consists of joining forces against a fellow student that doesn't conform to the group or against an especially difficult teacher. Children are kept in their own age groups and discouraged from making friends with anyone outside of that group. The goal becomes getting into or staying out of a certain clique. It is a given that adults are the enemy and not to be trusted.

Most teenagers experience feelings of inadequacy and believe they are the only ones feeling insecure about who they are. Experts say that building up a child's level of self-esteem will counteract the insecurity, but the typical teenager goes through these periods regardless of their level of self-esteem. Laurie went through this phase even though peer influence in general didn't seem to affect her. She wondered if she measured up to the other kids her age, although her worries mostly concerned her lack of mathematical abilities and her indecision about her future and less on her appearance. I remembered my own awkwardness at her age and was thankful that she was able to work through her feelings without hundreds of eyes upon her. I watched her struggle with her thoughts and wondered how long it would take her to feel confident with herself once again. I knew that it had taken me years to feel good about myself. I was pleasantly surprised to see her self-confidence return within a matter of months. Her body had adjusted to the hormonal changes and she was ready to take on new challenges. Throughout the years, people have commented favorably about the beauty of Laurie's self-confidence and told me they wish they had her attitude towards life.

One afternoon at college I was sitting on a bench reading a book while waiting for Laurie to get out of class. I looked up to see her coming out of a building, smiling and greeting people with a high-five, a quick hug or a "Hey, how's it going?" This group of people included a young Nigerian nun, a punk-looking guy with pink hair, a jock with a Nike jumpsuit, a lesbian couple and a middle-aged, distinguished looking man. Watching from a distance and seeing this diverse group of people each gladly returning Laurie's greetings made me proud, but also gave me cause to chuckle. I thought of how many times I had been asked, "How will she learn to socialize?" The negative tone of their voices insinuated that I was being an irresponsible parent. How I would love for those people to see her on the college campus.

Laurie's social life began long before her college days, however. The neighborhood children saw her as a leader and role model. On weekends and after school, they came to our house to spend time with Laurie. She would play with them until they started bickering among themselves, then she'd ask them to leave. As she and her friends entered their teen years, the attention of the other girls turned to "cute boys" and Laurie was disillusioned. She gradually distanced herself from the girls and got more involved with the computer. Her male cousin, Asher, was her best friend and they would spend summers together playing on computers and console games and reading books. She made new friends who were involved with the computer and showed no interest in dating until she was seventeen. After a short period of dating, she turned her full attention back to her studies.

Laurie's friends were not limited to her age range. She enjoyed friendships with adults and younger children also. She was not asked to leave the room when adult friends visited. Laurie was interested in the topics we discussed and supplemented the conversation with logical input. One of our friends has a degree in English and enjoys creative writing. Laurie enjoyed writing short stories, so our friend offered to critique her work for her. Laurie accepted and they spent hours going over ideas and writing styles.

Most adults enjoyed being around Laurie because she was not intimidated by them and participated in the conversation on equal terms. She was well read on various topics and always had something to say. If she was uninformed about the topic, she listened with interest. She often preferred the company of adults because she was interested in what was being said. However, some adults were intimidated by her maturity. They were not accustomed to having a sincere conversation with a child and it paralyzed them. They would ask her a school-type question, then start fidgeting when she replied earnestly. One woman told me that Laurie made her uncomfortable because she seemed too intelligent. The woman patronized Laurie and did not receive a typical childish response. I believe it was Laurie's perceptiveness and not her intellect that bothered the woman.

We did not force Laurie into social situations. Any interactions were natural and her choice. If she wanted to be alone, she asked the neighborhood friends to go home without any feedback from us about being rude. She enjoyed her solitude and still does. Now, at age twenty-two, Laurie has close friends and continues to enjoy friendships with people of all ages. A lack of school in her life did not hinder socialization;

rather, it broadened her acceptance of people far beyond the scope of classroom walls.

Skeptics

"A skeptic is a person who, when he sees the handwriting on the wall, claims it is a forgery."

~Morris Bender~

The majority of my family members took a neutral stance where unschooling was concerned. Although they did not support what I was doing they kept their opinions to themselves for the most part. They thought this was just another one of my nontraditional ideas that I would lose interest in and then Laurie would go to school. They believed that I should attend college and become a schoolteacher like my sister did and that Laurie should be in school like all other children. They were concerned about math and science and my dad would attempt to interest her in his many science books. He would ask school-type questions to see if she knew the basics. I am sure that my family was a bit perplexed and somewhat worried about Laurie. When she started college and not only loved it but made excellent grades, they were so proud and pleased because to them that signified success.

One of my proudest moments was when my mom, Laurie and I were sitting at the dining table discussing Laurie's love of college. Mom looked at me and said, "How did you know?" That one question validated what I had done for the past eighteen years. It more than validated my actions; it made me feel that my mom was saying, "We were all wrong about this. We thought you were nuts but you were right." The positive results were becoming obvious even to the skeptics.

My in-laws were supportive of unschooling from the beginning. They are intellectual people who learned beyond what the schools taught by reading on their own time. I will always be grateful for their support and for my sister-in-law Rebecca giving me the book that started all of this, Summerhill.

Some friends of ours that were homeschooling their children wanted to follow my example and unschool. The father's parents were so against natural learning that they threatened to turn my friends in to the school board office if they stopped 'teaching' their children at home. I am not sure what I would have done if I had been faced with this situation, but I would not have let it stop me. I would have found a way to continue unschooling, no matter what it took. When the grandmother of one of Laurie's friends found out how she had been raised, she asked her grandson, "Why did her mom want her to be stupid?" After meeting Laurie she realized how mistaken she was for assuming Laurie's intelligence level was low simply because she did not attend school.

My point is that you have to believe in yourself and your child enough to disregard the fears of others. My friend Jackie said it best: "Go forward with the dream you have in your heart and don't let someone else's fears slow you down." If I had taken all of the negative comments to heart about unschooling I would surely have put Laurie in school. Standing my ground on this decision has been the best thing I have ever done in my life. I have no regrets.

There may be times when you have doubts yourself about raising your child to be free. I was fortunate enough to have never dealt with doubt in Laurie or unschooling. One thing that helped was John Holt's newsletter, Growing Without Schooling. It made me realize that I was not alone with my beliefs to hear what others were going through while they were homeschooling their children. Having a support group is helpful even if it is thousands of miles away. There are now discussion groups online that deal exclusively with unschooling topics of concern.

When I say the word "unschooling," people generally assume I mean homeschooling, but the two are completely different. Homeschoolers generally follow a curriculum, bringing schoolwork into the home. One or both of the parents teaches and the children sit around a table or at a desk and do as they would in school. They believe that children can be taught more and of a better quality than is being taught at school. They generally feel that the routine and assessments are necessary to let them know if their child is on an average level with schooled children. While I would choose homeschooling over sending a child to school, homeschooling parents bring traditional school protocol into the home and make the home less friendly. Some homeschoolers try forced learning but later they relax and do not take the bookwork so seriously.

There were many homeschoolers in our area but no unschoolers that I was aware of. The homeschooling group met once a month at a recreational park so that the children could play together and the parents could discuss any problems they were having. Laurie and I attended a few of the meetings but found no like-minded people. The coordinator of the meetings knew that I was unschooling and she was very interested in how it was working. She asked me if I would speak about it at the next meeting. I agreed and was a bit excited at the prospect of sharing with others.

I was not prepared for the hostility and contempt with which they reacted. Laurie and I were basically shunned from the homeschoolers' meeting. Several of the women sitting closest to me fired questions at me, "What about math? Why aren't you teaching her math and science? You are making a big mistake." The anger in their voices baffled me. I told the crowd that I had faith that Laurie would learn what she needed to learn when necessary. I was met with frowns, smirks and looks of disgust.

I am not trying to make a political point or reject the beliefs of others but the young children of the women who were hostile about my parenting methods were wearing pro-life t-shirts with pictures of aborted fetuses on them.

There are things in your life that you never forget and seeing two and three-year olds with those shirts on will haunt me forever, because in my opinion that was child abuse. Those children cannot understand the abortion issues behind those pictures, yet there will be someone that confronts them about the shirts and they will end up having to deal with the issues of their parents.

One woman out of over one hundred adults approached me to ask more about unschooling after I sat down. We became friends but she decided to continue homeschooling her son and he eventually went to a private school. The homeschooling meeting continued with comments about schools being too lax and that strict discipline was necessary to raise children properly in today's permissive world. The comment was made that if teachers were allowed to use paddles again they would consider sending their children back to school because it would put a stop to the unruliness. Laurie and I left quietly and never returned to another meeting. Fifteen years later I called and left several messages asking if I would be allowed to speak at a meeting but no one returned my call. I assume that the members are still unenlightened and close-minded.

Another group that was hostile at the idea that I was keeping Laurie out of school was complete strangers. We did not stay home during the day so we heard the "Why isn't she in school?" question many times. We thought it best to say 'homeschooled' rather than have to explain what unschooling was or have someone call the authorities about what we were doing. I knew that some day I would not have to hide the unschooling lifestyle, but until it was more accepted I did not want to risk having Laurie's rights taken away from her.

Even the reply of 'homeschooling' was met with shock and anger. Some would tell me that what I was doing was illegal. I would explain that it was legal and they would then say that it was just wrong to not send my child to school. Instead of arguing with these people I simply smiled and we went on with our shopping. One woman in the grocery store asked the oft-asked question. I replied that Laurie was homeschooled and she blurted out with a snarl, "You are ruining her life!" I am not sure what those people thought was so evil about homeschooling but I was not going to respond to them in their state of mind. Imagine their hostility if I had informed people that Laurie did anything she wanted to do all day.

Others were less vicious but a bit shocked by what I was doing. An acquaintance asked, "How can you stand being around your kid all day? I would go insane." I replied that I thought it best that she not unschool her child if she did not like spending time with her. Things have a way of changing though. She phoned me several years later to ask me how she could take her child out of school because school had become a nightmare for her daughter. The mother's compassion overruled her need to be alone all day. I was thrilled to help her.

I think about the ignorance of people in regard to unschooling and know that by writing this book I will be setting Laurie and myself up for more hostility and rudeness but we are prepared to answer all questions and hopefully a few eyes will be opened. This is a beautiful and loving way to nurture your child and gives them a head start in life far superior to anything else you can do. I am also hoping that our exposure will allow present and future unschoolers to be able to talk about what they are doing more openly and help this wonderful lifestyle become more accepted.

Legal Issues

"Nothing strengthens authority so much as silence."

~Charles De Gaulle~

Our school board office was fairly cooperative with homeschoolers and with issuing private school status to individuals. We applied once a year to homeschool when Laurie was younger. In this application we had to supply some of her schoolwork in the different subjects, lists of field trips we had taken and books that she had read. For the curriculum I purchased a workbook that covered every subject for the first through the sixth grade. I tore out a page from each subject and helped Laurie fill in the correct answers. It did not matter to me if Laurie knew the answers and it certainly did not matter to her. We were satisfying the demands of a school board that we did not feel had a right to demand anything from us. Doing this once a year kept them happy and out of our lives. When Laurie was around ten years old I found out about registering our home as a private school. I registered and all of the hassles of a yearly application were removed.

In the state of Louisiana it was incredibly simple to register your home as a private school. Laurie made up a name for the school, created a letterhead on her computer for the school and typed in the necessary information. All that was needed was the school name, address, principal's name, teacher's name and number of students. Laurie's dad was named the principal and I the teacher with one student. This was sent in once a year until Laurie was sixteen, the legal age a child can drop out of school, as a formality to inform the school board of our private school status. Once we became a private school the school board had no say about how or what we taught. This simplified our lives immensely. Our Holt-Neill High School was no longer subject to the demands of the public school system.

I do not know all of the legal procedures for the different states or countries but do not listen to people that tell you it cannot be done. John Holt's books, the Growing Without Schooling newsletter and numerous websites can explain the legal requirements.

Mentors

"Feeling grateful or appreciative of someone or something in your life actually attracts more of the things that you appreciate and value into your life."

~Northrup Christiane~

There were many adults in Laurie's life that she looked up to in addition to her dad and me. She had grandparents, aunts, uncles and adult friends. However there is one person that stands out as a mentor to Laurie. Dr. Reba Rowe, her first sociology teacher, was not associated with our family and Laurie bonded with her immediately. I will never forget the excitement on her face when she came out of the building after the first class with Reba. "Sociology is SO cool, and Dr. Rowe is SO awesome!" She then quoted the notes from the entire class without looking at her notebook. That class and Dr. Rowe had made a lasting impression on Laurie and she soon realized that sociology was one of her passions.

Over the next few years Reba became more than a professor to Laurie; they became close friends. Reba and I also became friends and I loved the idea that Laurie was spending time with this wonderful woman. Soon Laurie became Reba's teaching assistant and helped her students who were having trouble understanding the work. Reba gave Laurie a key to her office and total trust.

Reba has been an important person in Laurie's life. She has been someone with whom Laurie shares a passion about sociology and someone outside of the family that believes in Laurie and has faith in her future. Thank you Reba, for being there for Laurie and sharing your passion with her.

There are other mentors in Laurie's life who have given her personal support. As I began thinking of the list of people, I realized that all of them are in the educational system. Is it ironic that she was unschooled and all of the people that she looks up to have careers with the system that I kept her out of? At first glance it would appear so. However, these people are in the college professorship field and that is very different from grade school. The public school teachers are concerned with truancy, homework, kids smoking on the school grounds and various other disciplinary problems that professors do not have to consider. College is not mandatory therefore the students generally want to be there.

Rebekah Griffith was our first math professor. She is such a talented teacher that she had us both loving math for the first time in our lives and we were able to understand all of the mathematical processes that she taught. Laurie liked Mrs. Griffith so much that she made sure to take her for the one statistics class that her major required. She loved the class so she went on to take upper-level statistics, including one just because Mrs. Griffith was teaching it. Laurie has taken three classes with Mrs. Griffith and they have become friends as well as student and teacher. Mrs. Griffith told me that Laurie, who was terrified of math at a young age, has a "gift" for the subject. Thank you Becky, for making such a difference in Laurie's life.

Dr. Delma McLeod-Porter was Laurie's Advanced Grammar and Composition professor. She admired Dr. Porter's teaching style from the beginning and was soon singing her praises at home. She recently told Dr. Porter that if she had been her professor in the earlier English classes that she might have majored in English. Dr. Porter has inspired Laurie to write and has been a friend to her. When I left Louisiana for several months, Dr. Porter proudly stepped in as "Surrogate Mom" and gave Laurie the support and encouragement that she needed. She spoke on Laurie's behalf in a meeting of an academic committee that culminated in Laurie receiving a scholarship. Thank you Delma, for lovingly taking my place and supporting Laurie's endeavors. Thank you also for the surrogate mom hugs you gave to her.

One other mentor that must be mentioned is Dr. Susan Kelso. Dr. Kelso was our professor for Introduction to Women's Studies. Laurie took a theatre class with Dr. Kelso one semester in which Laurie co-wrote her first starring role. Dr. Kelso gave her much support and praise for that accomplishment. Laurie had an independent study with Dr. Kelso during the following summer semester, which she greatly enjoyed because of the focused instruction. Thank you Susan, for all that you have done for Laurie.

All of the women that are special to Laurie have inspired her with their enthusiasm about their occupations. They are passionate about what they do which comes through in their speaking and in their lectures. Laurie is drawn to strong people who are content with what they are doing with their lives. Most of us are drawn to kindred spirits and I admire and respect Laurie's choices.

I feel certain that there are other mentors in Laurie's future because her ability to communicate with adults since childhood has perpetuated as she herself comes into adulthood. I remember being intimidated by adults as a child and even as a young adult myself. I did not trust them to see me as a potential peer but rather as a child without sensibilities. A change in parenting style can change the perceptions that adults and children have of each other and narrow future generation gaps.

Conclusion

A baby isn't born knowing what society expects of him. He starts learning from the moment he takes his first breath. With that first cry he has established himself as part of this universe. The cry does not have to be forced from him with a slap on his bottom. It happens naturally. If he is allowed to grow and learn naturally from then on, he will reach far past what his parents could possibly imagine.

A child does not have to be motivated to learn; in fact, learning cannot be stopped. A child will focus on the world around him and long to understand it. He will want to know why things are the way that they are. He won't have to be told to be curious; he will just be curious. He has no desire to be ignorant; rather he wants to know everything. But he wants to discover his interests on his own. He doesn't want to be pushed into learning what others think he should know. He wants to sample all that is in front of him and find his own destiny. Without interference he will do just that.

A baby comes into the world totally dependent on adults to survive. The power that a parent possesses from the time of a child's birth is profound. When a woman gets pregnant there is no way she can possibly fathom the impact her parenting choices will make on her child's life. Is she already putting her child onto a society-built pedestal that must crumble before the child can become independent? Does she see her child as a polite honor student that always does as he is told? Has she come to the mistaken conclusion that a polite and docile child is proof that she is a good mother? Has this conclusion been formed by blindly accepting what others around her have said about the children who are unwilling to "behave?"

Or does she not form conclusions about how her child will fit into society? Is it conceivable that she would want her future child to be a strong independent nonconformist? If she sees her child as someone who might make an enormous contribution to society, does she have the vaguest clue about what to do to insure his ability to do this? If she finds out that giving her child the best childhood he could possibly have will go against all the parenting rules she has ever heard of, will she have the courage to go through with it? Can she stand up to others for the sake of her child's welfare? Will her child come first, or will she break down and follow along like a "good" parent?

If you are an average citizen, you are unaware of the reality of today's society and you might not realize that being a "good" parent is one of the most oppressive things you can do to your child. It's highly unlikely that anyone cares about your child as an individual. Oh, they will say they care. They will pat him on the back when he brings home a good report card. They will praise him when he says "yes ma'am" and "no ma'am." But will it ever occur to them that these pats of praise are patronizing him in hopes that he will continue following the straight and narrow path of docility? They are congratulating your child on being the type of child that is more of a convenience for his parents. They are encouraging him to "make his parents proud." Would they praise him if he understood all of the inner workings of an airplane engine but flunked arithmetic?

Would the F on his report card be more important than his knowledge and enthusiasm over something he chose to learn about? Would he be told that knowing how to build an engine would not get him a diploma and would he be discouraged and ridiculed every time he excitedly mentioned his latest discovery about jet fuels? Would these same people think it was incredible for him to originate an idea that would make faster and safer planes only after he made good grades in school? They do not care about your child as a unique individual. They only care that he fits in to society and does not embarrass them in front of others. Their values are superficial and more harmful than most people can mentally grasp.

So what does a newly conscientious parent do? First of all, read books about unschooling and natural learning. There is a list in the back of this book. Commit your life to your child or children with no regard to parenting rules that are archaic and detrimental to the family. Forget about looking for a "good" traditional school. There are none. Any institution that gives higher value to discipline and grades is going to be harmful to your child. Realize that by deciding to have a child, you must do what is in the best interest of that child. But don't see your parental role as one of self-sacrifice and bondage. Embrace parenthood and see it as a choice that you made. Take fifteen to twenty years to see the world through the eyes of your child and learn more than you ever thought possible. Lose the power trip mentality and be a friend to your child. There is no career promotion that can come close to the camaraderie between you and your child when your child knows that you truly trust and respect him.

How can you become a trusting and respectful parent? By letting go of the traditional authoritative rules that are being lauded as the best way to raise a child. Think about why you are enforcing a rule. Is it to keep your child on a certain path that you manipulate with demands and expectations? Is it so that your living room stays neat and orderly with no sign of being lived-in? Or is the rule enforced simply because it's a rule your parents had when raising you? Unless the rule is for personal safety of your child and/or another person, then the rule should be forgotten. Even those rules need to be thoroughly examined to make sure you are not being overprotective. See your child as an individual instead of a small person who is incapable of making a decision. Realize that your child was not born in order to fulfill your need to "own" a perfect example of a human.

If you erase the boundaries associated with traditional parenting your child will mature much quicker. If he is never treated as less important than the adults and never put into a school situation, the learning process that began at birth will continue steadfastly throughout his entire life. He won't have to lose a minimum of twelve years of his life trying to figure out what everyone else expects of him. Instead he will be busy striving to become the person he was naturally intended to be. He won't waste time memorizing facts and at times untruths, so that he can pass a test on topics that have no interest to him whatsoever. It doesn't matter where his interests lie. It's not your right to determine his life's work. He will figure out what he wants to do with his life in his own due time. He will push harder, reach farther and be more dedicated to his choice of study.

You cannot stop him from being the person he wants to be. You might succeed in postponing his triumph by putting many obstacles and hurdles in his path, but eventually he will arrive at his chosen destination. What a tragedy it would be if you succeeded in guilt-tripping your child into becoming a surgeon when he wanted to be an architect. Even if he managed to hide his discontent and resentment of your manipulations, the truth would come out. He would remain a surgeon and know all of his adult life that he was not doing what he wanted to do or he would find a way to become an architect. Wouldn't it have been much simpler for both of you if you had just supported him to go in whatever direction he chose to go?

That support begins at birth. It's doubtful that an infant knows his future profession, but allowing him to make decisions about his feeding times, sleeping times and when he's held are ways in which you can help him become independent. When he gets a little older and wants to wear his rubber boots to a funeral, you have another chance at letting him shape his own identity. Would that be a difficult thing for you to allow? If you said "Yes" then ask yourself "Why?" Would it be difficult because of the embarrassment you would feel because your child is the only one there not wearing "appropriate" clothing? Are you more concerned about what other people think of you than you are about your own child's feelings? Look deeper at situations like this. Don't see it as your child being defiant and weird. See him as a strong person separate from you and your opinions of proper attire. See him as an individual making his own choice about what he wears. What about the woman who is looking distastefully at your son's boots? Is her opinion more important than your son's? Why should she have any influence over how your child dresses? Why should anyone? Believe me, it's easier to smile and be proud of your decision to raise an emotionally healthy child. And if it rains at the cemetery, your son will be the only person with the correct footwear.

There are many instances every day like the one described above that give you the chance to let go and allow your child the freedom to grow strong, independent and self-confident. Will the rubber boots matter ten years from now? If your child wearing rubber boots to a funeral has any bearing on his success in life, it will be a positive one. He will know all of his life that his mother and/or father trusted him to make his own decisions in every circumstance. He'll most likely even ask for your honest opinion about his choices in life. Isn't this worth far more than the price of a little embarrassment at a long-forgotten funeral?

There is so much irony involved in the two types of parenting. The authoritative parent wants a well-mannered child who does what he's told, makes good grades in class and never gets into trouble. He wants his child to submit to authority while standing up against peers who would get him into trouble. He wants his child to make good grades, be a team leader in sports and conduct himself respectfully. To be certain that his child follows the course that's been laid out for him, he sets guidelines, makes rules and enforces them with stern looks, threats and/or spankings. He believes that if he is strict enough, his child will "turn out well." The expected results are seldom achieved. Often when it appears that the results are favorable, it is only an illusion painstakingly created by the child and/or the parent. Herein lies the irony.

If the parent relinquishes authority over the child and allows him to grow naturally, he is more likely to "turn out well" than if he was coerced. Not only will the outcome be positive, but it will surpass the majority. The child who has led his own learning possesses a holistic perspective on life. He is well-mannered but has no qualms about standing up for what he believes. As a rule he is well-read in his chosen field, non-judgmental, confident, has morals and is not introverted. He will not go along with the crowd unless he has determined that the crowd is moving in the right direction. His success might tempt you to say how proud you are of him, but all you should be proud of is stepping back and letting him grow. He has very few, if any, hangups to overcome because you succeeded in removing unnecessary obstacles from his life.

I am not an authority on parenting or unschooling. I do not have a college degree that shows the world my level of education. I do have a twenty-three year old daughter, Laurie, whom I unschooled all of her life. I wrote this book to help others make the decision to keep their child out of the school system and away from the unnecessary control over their child's life. In a home where the adults are not the absolute authority, life is less stressful and more fun for everyone. The children aren't breaking rules because there are none. No one is seeing to it that orders have been obeyed and doling out punishments. A clock or the amount of homework does not control life. Since the parents are not constantly overseeing the behavior of their children, they now have the time to pursue their own interests. The amazing thing is that their children are so enjoyable to be around, that the parents want to be with them. When other parents are searching for ways to get away from their children for a few hours, you will be making plans with your children.

I hope my book helps you take that step that will better your life in more ways than you can imagine. I wish all parents would create an atmosphere conducive to being friends with their children. Rebellious would become a term that no longer applied to teenagers. Prisons would have empty cells and therapist would not be a household word. Children would grow up and leave home and have no apprehension about coming home to visit. Young adults would know what they want and work towards that goal with courage. Does this sound like something from a work of science fiction? It's not. It's easily attained with the adjustment of parental attitudes.

Books I Recommend:

Appleton, Matthew. *A Free Range Childhood: Self-Regulation at Summerhill School.* Foundation for Education Renewal.

Dyer, Dr. Wayne W. *Your Erroneous Zones.* Funk & Wagnalls.

Freire, Paulo. *Pedagogy of the Oppressed.* Continuum Publishing Corporation.

Gardner, Howard. *The Unschooled Mind: How Children Think & How Schools Should Teach.* BasicBooks.

Gatto, John Taylor. *A Different Kind of Teacher: Solving the Crisis of American Schooling.* Berkeley Hills Books.

Gatto, John Taylor. *Dumbing Us Down: The Hidden Curriculum of Compulsory Schooling.* New Society Publishers.

Gatto, John Taylor. *The Exhausted School: Bending the Bars of Traditional Education.* Berkeley Hills Books.

Griffith, Mary. *The Unschooling Handbook: How to Use the Whole World As Your Child's Classroom.* Prima Publishing.

Hern, Matt. *Deschooling Our Lives.*

243

Holt, John. *How Children Fail*. Perseus Publishing.

Holt, John. *How Children Learn*. Perseus Publishing.

Holt, John. *Learning All the Time*. Perseus Publishing.

Hunt, Jan and Peggy O'Mara. *The Natural Child: Parenting from the Heart*. New Society.

Illich, Ivan. *Deschooling Society*. Marion Boyars Publishers.

Kozol, Jonathan. *Savage Inequalities: Children in America's Schools*. Harper Perennial.

Leonard, George. *Education and Ecstasy*. North Atlantic Books.

Llewellyn, Grace. *Real Lives: Eleven Teenagers Who Don't Go to School*. Lowry House.

Llewellyn, Grace. *The Teenage Liberation Handbook: How to Quit School and Get a Real Life and Education*. Lowry House.

Llewellyn, Grace and Amy Silver. *Guerilla Learning: How to Give Your Kids a Real Education With or Without School*. John Wiley & Sons.

Neill, A.S. *Summerhill School: A New View of Childhood.* St. Martin's Press.

Orr, Tamra *A Parent's Guide to Home Schooling*

Orr, Tamra *Things Homeschoolers Can Do On The Internet*

Pearce, Joseph Chilton. *Evolution's End: Claiming the Potential of Our Intelligence.* Harper San Francisco.

Pearce, Joseph Chilton. *Magical Child: Rediscovering Nature's Plan for Our Children.* E.P. Dutton.

Reimer, Everett W. *School is Dead: An Essay On Alternatives In Education.* Penguin.

Rogers, Carl. *Freedom to Learn.* Charles E. Merrill Publishing Company.

Sheffer, Susannah. *A Sense of Self: Listening to Homeschooling Adolescent Girls.* Boynton/Cook.

Wimsatt, William Upski. *No More Prisons.* Soft Skull Press.

Please see our website at

www.ubpub.com

for updated links to unschooling sites